O. A. Battista, Sc.D.

PEOPLE
POWER

(RSC)
RESEARCH SERVICES CORPORATION
BOOK PUBLISHING DIVISION
FORT WORTH, TEXAS 76133

FOR WRITTEN PERMISSIONS
AND ALL SUBSIDIARY
RIGHTS

WRITE

Research Services Corporation
Permissions Department
P.O. Drawer 16549
Fort Worth, Texas 76133

BATTISTA, O. A.
PEOPLE POWER
Library of Congress Catalog Card No. 76-58684
ISBN: 0915074-07-9

PEOPLE POWER

by O. A. BATTISTA

What do you want others to do for you?

Would you like the other fellow to do *more* for you *more* willingly? Co-operate with you on a special project? Help you with a difficult problem or an unexpected emergency? Buy more of your products? Do a better job for you? See and support your decision? The simple techniques disclosed in this book are sure-fire ways to get the other fellow on your side and keep him there.

In these pages, a well-known leader, author and scientist shows you 1) why people act *toward you* the way they do, and 2) where the master keyboard of their instincts and emotions lie, and 3) how you can most effectively control or influence this keyboard in a wholesome manner.

For instance, you see how to influence the other fellow's ego to win his *eager* co-operation, his respect and his full support. You learn the camouflaged part that pride plays in determining his attitudes — his actions — his sense of loyalty — his desire to "belong." You find out how to evoke favorable emotional responses through special techniques of suggestion. Herein you have presented a unique array of specific words, phrases and ideas which possess an almost magical power to influence or lead the minds of others.

In your *family relations,* this book teaches you a tested art of achieving lasting peace and harmony; but it also teaches you how to say NO without damaging cooperation in any way.

In your *business affairs,* this book is a right-hand assistant for the ambitious employee who wants to get ahead — for the salesman who wants more customers — for the manager or leader who wants to spur his staff to greater effort. It shows how to win an argument and a friend; how to criticize others without forfeiting their goodwill; how to make a man equate his company's best interests with his own personal best interests.

As Andrew Carnegie once said, "It marks a big step in your development when you come to realize that other people can help you do more than you could do alone." The truth of this statement applies in every walk of life. This book proves it beyond question by revealing case histories and by showing you how to put other people on your team *all* the way.

ABOUT THE AUTHOR

What makes people "tick"? How can you influence them in positive ways? These are the two questions around which Dr. Battista started this book. After making a check-list of his own techniques and experiences, he asked these questions of hundreds of business, professional and social leaders. Out of this vast wealth of material has emerged this new book on human relations.

O. A. Battista was Vice President for Science and Technology, AVICON, Inc., until 1974. He then became Special Consultant to AVICON, and Chairman of the Board and President of RESEARCH SERVICES CORPORATION. He is a graduate of McGill University and has received 64 U.S. patents and more than 450 foreign patents. His discoveries include Avicel® microcrystalline cellulose, which now has annual sales in millions of pounds for use in pharmaceuticals and low-calorie foods, and AVICON's Avitene® microfibrillar collagen, a unique hemostat-adhesive for surgery. Dr. Battista has published more than 80 scientific papers, has pioneered the new field of microcrystal polymer chemistry, and is the author of 17 books and hundreds of articles for foremost magazines. He received the Grady Gold Medal Award of the American Chemical Society, is a member of many professional societies, and recipient of numerous honors. Adjunct Professor of Chemistry, and Director, Center for Microcrystal Polymer Science, University of Texas, Arlington, Texas, he also is president of the American Institute of Chemists.

PEOPLE POWER

BOOKS
by
O. A. Battista

How To Enjoy Work and GET More Fun Out of Life   *(Prentice-Hall)*
God's World and You   *(Bruce)*
The Challenge of Chemistry   *(Holt, Rinehart & Winston)*
The Power to Influence People   *(Prentice-Hall)*
Commonscience in Everyday Life   *(Bruce)*
Mental Drugs: Chemistry's Challenge to Psychotherapy   *(Chilton)*
Toward the Conquest of Cancer   *(Chilton)*
Fundamentals of High Polymers   *(Reinhold)*
Synthetic Fibers in Papermaking   *(Wiley)*
Microcrystal Polymer Science   *(McGraw-Hill)*
A Dictionary of QUOTOONS   *(RSC Corporation)*
CHILDISH QUESTIONS (with H. K. Battista)   *(RSC Corporation)*
Research For Profit   *(RSC Corporation)*
Work For Profit   *(RSC Corporation)*
People Power   *(RSC Corporation)*
Speaker's Dictionary of Quotoons   *(RSC Corporation)*
Olympiad of Knowledge, 1984   *(RSC Corporation)*

★   ★   ★   ★   ★   ★

SERVICE TO OUR READERS

The above books, as well as ANY BOOK and any PERIODICAL on ANY subject published anywhere in the world may be obtained from a single source — RESEARCH SERVICES CORPORATION, Post Office Drawer 16549, Fort Worth, Texas 76133, 817/292-4270.

To

MARY ELIZABETH KEFFER

Contents

vii

12. The Ten Principles of Influencing and Dealing with People (Cont.)

PEOPLE POWER

1.

The Most Important Person
in Your Life

IT IS A PROVEN FACT! ONE OF YOUR MOST DEEP-rooted desires in life is to have the power to influence people and to get along well with others. The simple but oft-neglected formula for moving ahead in life still is to get other people to push for you, to "be on your side" all the way! If you already are striving to apply this formula in your life, the chances are you not only are headed in the right direction but are well along the way to the top, too. You already may have begun to cash in on the fact that the best way to get ahead is to use your power to influence other people.

Getting to know and like people, and getting people to know and like you, are the trump cards in the game of success. They can lead you to the kind of life that everyone hopes and dreams of but all too few enjoy to the full.

YOUR KEY TO POWER AND INFLUENCE WITH PEOPLE
You Can't Do It All by Yourself

"It marks a big step in a man's development," Andrew Carnegie once confided to a close friend, "when you come to realize

1

that other people can help you do a better job than you could do alone." This truth is a milestone marking the turning point in the development of successful human relations since Carnegie's day. Realize the importance of "other people" in your life, and the fact that "other people" hold your destiny—and mine—like a ball of molding clay in their hands, and you will take your first big step on the road to success and happiness. Your next step comes when you know how to get other people to help you reach your goal.

Modern psychology has not discovered a more effective guide to success in influencing people than the time-tested Golden Rule: treat others *first* the way you hope they will treat you later. A day-to-day practice of this great rule, a day-to-day emphasis on the needs and emotions of others, will give you full confidence and greater power in your dealings with people. It also will bring to you more than enough success to make you happy and satisfied with your lot in life.

To put this principle another way, try treating the other person as though you knew he held your destiny in his hands. The results are sure to astonish him and please you!

It may go against your way of thinking to admit that what you become in life, how many of life's blessings, of life's rich and satisfying rewards you are able to acquire, depend far less on what *you* do than on what the other person does *for* or *to* you. It may be startling for you to think that your future is like putty in the hands of others. Yet it is a facing up to this forceful truth that can make or break you. Happiness, self-satisfying pleasures, financial success, and prestige among your fellowmen are yours only if you are able to get others to help you to achieve them.

William James, America's greatest psychologist, tried to put this basic truth in a six-word nutshell: "Human relations are the main thing." What he was trying to tell us was that the biggest, most vital thing in your life and mine is to learn through self-discipline how to get along happily with our fellow human beings. No commodity in the business or social world today is as valuable as the ability to gain the support and cooperation you must have from others to enjoy life and be an outstanding success.

For example, even Theodore Roosevelt, a man whose wealth and depth of human understanding remains an immortal monument to his lofty stature, found that he could not succeed alone. He discovered eventually that he could muster a hundred times more backing by getting other people, those with the best qualifications in those areas in which he himself was weak, to cooperate with him.

He said on one occasion: "I stood out for my own opinion alone. I took the best mugwump stand. My own conscience, my own judgments were to decide in all favors. I would listen to no arguments, no advice. Finally, I learned that with the things I really wanted to do, however, I was powerless to accomplish them alone." If as great a man as Theodore Roosevelt had to wait until late in life to realize how helpless he was without the help of others, how much more important it is for you and me to recognize now that the other fellows, with whom you must live on this earth, are really the important people in your life. These are the people who must receive first consideration from you before you can sway others, command their actions and reactions, make them compete for the honor of serving your wishes.

Greatness today no longer comes from the deep, strong manners of the lone wolf or the tyrant. The great strong men of history have disappeared along with the horse and buggy. Today the man who gives service, who dedicates his whole being to others, and executes the will of the people in a way that pleases them most, emerges with the gift of greatness and the reward of true power.

Today, your best pathway to popularity and great success lies in your ability to submerge yourself in the current of the other person's needs and feelings. Merely "getting along with people" is not enough. You must *give* of yourself to *get* for yourself. One of the finest lawyers I know is a man who becomes completely absorbed in each case that he handles. The accountant who keeps my financial records in order handles them with as much interest in my behalf as if they were his very own. This is the kind of unselfish devotion to service that endears you lastingly to others.

The people who influence my life the most (probably the same is true also of the influential people in your life), without exception, are the ones who go out of their way to make me feel important. They have me in their power in the sense that, willingly and enthusiastically, I will exert my best efforts in their behalf!

The Best Way to Deal with Everyone

Taking, then, as the nexus of your life the realization of the practical value to you of harmonious dealings with other people, you can easily revamp many of your ideas on human relations. Start by setting up a few ground rules in order to place the other fellow in a relatively new and even elevated position with respect to your own ego. The best way to deal with *all* people is to remember that they are made the same way you are, subject to similar doubts, spells of reserve, and hesitancies. They, too, must be "thawed out." Each time you succeed in getting through to the warm goodwill that radiates from a person, even though sometimes his outward actions make you think there's no goodwill there, you take a big step up the ladder to success in your dealings with people.

Almost every year, one important poll or another reports that employers without exception place greatest emphasis on a particular human ability above all others. That ability, which has the greatest pulling power both in terms of paycheck and progress up the ladder, is *the ability to get along with others.* Why does this technique command premium pay in so many different spheres of living? It is because, in everyday practice, the successful handling of other people calls for more self-control and self-analysis than the average person is willing to exercise. It also is the proven yardstick which governs the productivity and the *esprit de corps* behind every team.

Men and women who have gotten to the top in life, in any field, had one quality in common: they got the things they wanted to have done through the willing efforts of other people. Their knack of doing this was always so simple: they worked calmly but with calculation to bring the best out of others without putting themselves too noticeably into the spotlight. They discovered the great truth that a hand outstretched in friendship, a personality radiating love and warmth for the other fellow, is the magic key, the "Open Sesame" to ever-increasing success and popularity. They learned to look at life and people with their heart instead of just their eyes. A heart full of goodwill toward your neighbor and your fellow man can do more to win the affection and support of people than any other known ability or trait. This is the rare and magical gift of leadership and popularity in its plainest garb.

A very successful president of a large American corporation told me, "Most of the other fellows I have known who failed were just as ambitious as I was. They certainly were endowed with as much intellectual go-power. But they did not do enough self-analysis to discover the rough spots in their make-ups, to smooth out the scratchy elements in their personalities. They did not even try to cultivate that very elusive quality about the human being that invites—literally seduces—other people to become interested in them. In my opinion, any person who knows how to treat others so they will want to be with you, to feel stimulated by doing things with or for you, has in his hands the magic key that will open the door to any goal he sets for himself."

Still another prominent executive offered me this seasoned advice, "Build up as many other people as you can. No greater dividends can come to you than the dividends you will receive from helping others to grow, even to grow past you."

Help to build up other persons so that they will become better, stronger, and finer people because of you. You must, of course, build up other people unselfishly by doing things for them because you want to. There is nothing wrong in this approach even when you may foresee possibilities for yourself if, through you, they are able to reach a higher level of success. It is this type of dedicated service toward your fellow man, the deliberate act of making *his* rather than *your* ego the object of your concern, that always will cause him to think well of you. Only then can you count on the kind of external support that is bound to guarantee your own progress and ever-widening influence with people.

One of the secrets of getting to understand the other fellow as a basis for mustering his interest and support is to appreciate the fact that it is a rare man indeed who doesn't wish he were somebody else. Unfortunately, as each of us grows into adulthood, many of the dreams that we had as youngsters, the bundles of possibilities that we may have entertained for our futures, become reduced to one or two alternatives. One by one our boyhood dreams fade away as we mature. Suddenly, the day arrives when we must choose a path for our life's career.

Frequently, practical considerations of the day determine what our choice will be. But, alas, seldom does our final decision measure up to the deep dreams we may have entertained in our youth. Consequently, the other person is always ready to believe or hope that he may yet become somebody else. This "somebody else" is like the grass in the other pasture; it still strikes his mind as being "greener or greater."

Once you learn the great power that the other fellow has over your destiny, power and influence for you become almost assured. It means that you will deliberately seek out the needs in other people's lives and then devotedly try to fill them. It means that you will become a comfortable person to be with, one with whom the other fellow can associate without any sense of strain. You, on the other hand, will thrill to new levels of pleasure and delight when you see how the other fellow responds to you with a warm feeling of agreement and sympathy.

I am sure you have on more than one occasion forced yourself to smile to bolster your own morale. So also you must use subtle "force" in the form of persuasiveness to get the other person to be friendly, cooperative, and determined to help you get more out of life. There isn't a person alive who doesn't crave love, companionship, creativeness, intellectual stimulation, and a thousand of the more everyday enjoyments of life. But in order to get the full measure of pleasure from these wonderful things you must inevitably share them with the other fellow. What is equally necessary is that the other person must want to do the sharing with you willingly.

Your Success Depends on How Others Back You Up

The reason, therefore, that others hold your destiny literally in their hands is that your happiness is dependent on *how* you, for your own part, go about trying to gain the love, respect, and backing of your family, your friends, and your associates.

Our personalities are but echos of our contacts with other people. In a practical sense, our day-to-day emotional stature is molded and shaped not by our hands but by the words and actions of others for or against us.

How else, for example, can we possibly explain the tremendous success and power which Will Rogers had in dealing with people. The hearts of people everywhere opened up to him like flowers to the morning. Why? The answer is given so clearly in one of his most popular statements: "I never met a man I did not like."

In my own experience, I have learned repeatedly that it is a sound, practical philosophy always to remember that it is much easier to get along with everyone than it is to get along with only one or two! Not until I learned to bow to the other fellow, to adjust to his idiosyncrasies, to mold my temperament to his, to block an argument, and to cultivate in its place understanding and agreement, did I make any progress in getting him to help make my destiny more favorable.

It Pays to Be Nice to People

Each minute, each hour, each day of your life you have the choice of getting the best or the worst out of the other person. It is only the attention you give the whisperings from your own conscience that can help you to decide the outcome of your actions.

Learn never to dislike people because they differ with you. Fight every urge to entertain discrimination because of conflicts of political or religious points of view. Develop a compassion for others based on the understanding that they suffer from the same fears and frustrations plaguing you. Never assume or believe that you have enemies even though the circumstantial evidence may tempt you to believe otherwise. You cannot really be nice as long as you allow a morsel of hate or distrust to disturb your direct contacts with others.

Give other persons full credit for holding your destiny in their hands; it is the surest way to get them to protect that destiny with the best qualities they can muster. When you must differ or take issue with another person, show him, by your looks and your words, by the palpable spirit of your conscience that you nevertheless love and respect him.

And, above all, to mold your destiny *through other persons* avoid, at all costs, the capital mistake of losing your temper and raising your voice. A man who "blows his top," no matter how justified it may be, builds a high-walled fence around his personality. I have known men, who, because they allowed themselves to "hit the ceiling" just once, have worked for years to regain the confidence and respect of their associates and their superiors.

Appeal to the loftier sentiments of others. Put consideration of others above consideration of yourself, especially when you do not have to. Develop the habit of forbearance; it is far more persuasive than any form of direct logic. Make it easy for the other person to say "yes" rather than "no" when he must make the decision for or against you.

A feeling of hate for the people who have done or are doing the most to help you get ahead is the mark of one doomed to tragic and certain failure. Rather, teach yourself to think highly of others and you will be amazed at how well they will take care of you. Yes, your key to the top most heights of achievement is like putty in the hands of others. That is why the other fellow holds your destiny in his hands far more than you know or believe.

2.

How to Get the Other Fellow
Behind You from the Start

"TO BEGIN IS HALF THE WORK," WROTE AUSONIUS. Paraphrasing this sage comment, you might say, "To make a good *first* impression is more than half the job of dealing successfully with people." Many a man now buried in the graveyard of failure tumbled because of the way he faced up to somebody the first time!

The way you "hit" people at first meeting often determines how they react to you for a long time to come. If you rub someone the wrong way the first time you meet and talk with him, it may take months, even years, to correct the initial reaction he has to your personality and aims. If you want to get people to back you up, you have to get them behind you right from the start.

Each time I weigh the great value of first impressions in human relations, I am reminded of a comment that a "Miss America" winner made some years ago. At her wedding a reporter asked her, "What was it that *first* attracted you to George over all the other men who dated you?" Her answer was unhesitant, and so logical. "His first kiss!" she replied. The effectiveness of first

9

kisses, alas, like first impressions, depends so heavily on whether or not the response is a "Come again," or "Drop dead, brother!"

WHEN A TOUCH OF HUMOR CAN SAVE THE DAY

A good friend of mine, Al, showed up at his office one morning with his left arm in a splint and sling. He had injured it the night before while ice skating. He knew he was going to have to present the full story of a new product he had developed to his company's Executive Committee this morning. It was the first time he had ever had to talk to so many vice presidents at one time. And, as he told me, "I *would* have to fracture my wrist the night before the crucial meeting!"

Al's problem was how to make a favorable first impression while looking like a lame duck. The solution came to him a few minutes before the meeting started. When he was called upon by his supervisor to tell his story, he got up and said, "Gentlemen, into each life some rain must fall. Last night some came into my life, but it turned into ice and I fell on it." Al's opening comment was ideal; it explained his accident and conditioned his audience favorably as he promptly launched into the story of the new product he had developed. Later he told me that the Executive Committee backed him and his product all the way. He was convinced he had opened their minds to accepting it by his first comment.

Humor can work wonders for you as it did for Al in all kinds of situations. Here are two guiding suggestions:

1. When you come home from work and find your wife in a serious or depressed mood, do or say something to get her or the children laughing; it can make all the difference between a happy or an unpleasant evening.
2. Your boss calls you into his office for a dressing down about a mistake you know you made. An introductory comment like, "When I make a mistake, I make a beaut! I'm sorry about this," may take away much of the sting.

On another similar occasion I recall how a bad first impression caused a man irreparable harm. He showed up at work with a black eye; one of his youngsters had booted him accidentally the night before when he was playing with him. This chap spent a good ten minutes explaining the "shiner" to a bored audience. The result was a bad first impression even before he got to the point of his talk.

All through life you will find that such split-second changes in mood or opinions or feelings in others, brought on largely by the first impression they have of you, may literally steer you to success or failure.

Use the following suggestions to protect yourself from making the kind of impressional *faux pas* that can handicap you:

1. Never start a conversation or open an introduction by highlighting some virtue of your own.
2. Never allow a conversation to center too heavily on yourself. Break it up so that the other person gets into the spotlight regularly.
3. Never give yourself a "black eye" by ever displaying anger, raising your voice, or taking a belligerent stand, especially when you are about to be faced by the facts of a situation or a problem for the first time.

A close friend of mine, Bill K., who is now a top industrial executive, told me how a first impression was the key to his rapid advancement up the ladder.

Shortly after he was granted his mechanical engineering degree from M.I.T., he was hired by a large Philadelphia corporation. Bill was the type of fellow who believed in learning by doing, no matter how hard or dirty the "doing" might be.

One day, as he was hard at work tearing apart an idle machine in the plant, the president of the company, along with Bill's boss, passed by on a routine plant inspection.

Bill K. was quite a sight at the time. He was in overalls and dirtier than a happy-go-lucky high school lad working as a "grease monkey" at a gas station. Except for the expression of intense interest in what he was doing, and an obvious air of delight with it, Bill looked a sight!

But the president of the firm was a hard-hitting executive who had worked up from the bottom; nobody caught his sharp eye faster than an employee at any level working like a beaver.

Bill K. noticed that the two men stopped for a moment beside the machine he was working on. Except for a smile and a nod toward his supervisor, however, he worked merrily away.

Bill did not know it at the time, but the "big boss" had stopped long enough to get the "vital statistics" about him from his supervisor. Some months later, when the president needed a mechanical engineer to serve as a staff assistant to him, Bill K. got the nod. As his supervisor explained to him when he broke the good news, "The boss sure was favorably impressed by you when he saw you for the first time in grease up to your neck and hard at work on that old machine."

This story points out one of the most valuable approaches to making a favorable first impression on the job; nothing speaks louder in your behalf with the men up the line than a conscientious and intensely interested "nose-to-the-grindstone" reputation. A "nose to the grindstone" reputation can be bolstered by such common sense actions on your part as these:

1. Adherence to office hours—make those coffee breaks ten minutes, not twenty-five—leave home five minutes sooner so that you get on the job ahead of the boss.
2. When you have a report to get done by a certain deadline, surprise your boss by getting it on his desk ahead of time, even if you have to do a little work on it at home.
3. When asked to do more than your regular job, do it promptly, willingly and thoroughly. There is no better recommendation when being considered for a higher job than an uncomplaining attitude towards an ever-increasing work load.
4. Don't be afraid to exercise enthusiasm when you recognize a good idea by another person; go all out to encourage its promotion.
5. Give as many of your associates as you can credit or help. There is no more genuine way to impress yourself on them.

The impression you leave during an interview for a job is also something that lingers for a lifetime. I have had occasion in my business life to recommend the employment of a large number of people. As I go over that list of those that I have hired, as well as quite a few that were rejected, I can vividly recall the favorable or unfavorable first impression which remain in my mind.

For example, I recall the attractive young lady who insisted on walking up the stairs to my office rather than taking the automatic elevator. She had an intense fear of elevators. This young lady proved to be emotionally immature; she did much better as a stockroom clerk than as a laboratory technician.

Or consider the college graduate who left me with a most unfavorable first impression. I have no idea where he is today or what he is doing, but I would be surprised if he is very successful. Within two minutes after our conversation began he asked me point blank, "With the name of 'Battista,' are you a relative of the fellow in Cuba?" My answer was an abrupt "No!" My first impression was a decidedly negative one.

Compare my response to this applicant with that to another one who got the job. The first impression that the second fellow gave me was enough to open my mind to his basic virtues. He came right out and said, "Dr. Battista, this is the first interview I have ever had. Won't you help me do a good job with it?" Such alarming honesty caused me to put my arm around this young college graduate's shoulder and help him out. His honesty and humility, combined with an admirable enthusiasm for doing well, carried this young man to a position in later years which far exceeded the post I enjoyed when I hired him originally.

THINGS TO DO DURING AN INTERVIEW

1. Listen!
2. Never ask questions too soon. The person who is interviewing you has a story to tell; don't interrupt him until he tells it. Besides, in this way you will avoid asking weak questions.
3. I'm always impressed by an interviewee who shows by his questions that he knows the company's financial position, that he has taken the time before the interview to get these facts and study them.
4. Discuss salaries frankly. It is your privilege to get these

facts when you start a job, your responsibility to see what happens to your salary *after* you get the job.

5. Avoid personal or personality chit-chat, unless it is encouraged by the other party. Then steer it only along the lines he or she is interested in. No one is more annoying than an interviewee who bores you with a breakdown of all his famous relatives.

INGENUITY CAN SOMETIMES TURN
THE TRICK FOR YOU

There are many success stories that follow the general pattern of the young man who, in a line of applicants, was worried that someone would be chosen for a given job before he even had a chance to be interviewed. Accordingly, he wrote a little note and asked one of the attendants to deliver it to the head man at the interviewing desk. The note simply said, "Please don't reach a decision until you have a chance to talk to the young man with a crew-cut who is close to the end of the line." Needless to say, the crew-cut applicant got the job because his initiative made a very favorable first impression. Simple as this may seem, this is exactly the kind of ingenuity that you should try to use on your own upward climb to the top.

Sometimes, when conditions are desperate enough, you make a good impression spontaneously. For instance, I once experienced a graphic illustration of the power of good first impressions. I was scheduled to make a speech in a town about 50 miles from my office. My time was tight and I was hurrying to make the engagement. Without fully realizing it, I was driving through a 35-mile-an-hour zone at 45 miles-an-hour. Suddenly, out of a parked car along a straight stretch, a state trooper stepped out and waved me down. Almost at once, I had visions of a stiff speeding summons, a harsh lecture from the trooper, and maybe even a long delay in a courtroom before a tough judge.

Resentment against the whole situation began to well up inside me. My first reaction was to become angry at the trooper for stopping me when I was in such a rush. Luckily, I thought twice before I put my foot into my mouth. This was the first time I had ever been stopped by a state trooper; I didn't know what to expect. But in a flash I realized that it didn't make any difference at all what I thought of that trooper; it was what the officer thought of me that counted. My best chance was to make a good impression on him, by a spur-of-the-moment attempt to make him aware that I honestly had no intention of breaking the speed limit and that I really was glad he stopped me before I got into more serious trouble.

So, not knowing what to expect, I rolled down my window and looked up at him with as friendly a smile as I could muster. I was resolved to like that trooper, and to make him like me, no matter what my punishment was to be! He approached me in a quiet, courteous manner; he was "the law" but there was none of that sinking feeling in the stomach that people often get when in spots like this. He asked me in a pleasant tone, "May I see your driver's license?"

Almost mechanically I produced my license. The trooper's manner had made such an impression on me that I found myself saying with real conviction something like this: "Officer, when you stopped me I thought I was going to be angry and I thought I was going to be scared. I'm late for an important meeting at which I am to speak, and I hate to be late for anything. I guess that's why I was doing more than the limit. I've never been stopped by a traffic officer before and I fully expected to be raked over the coals. But you haven't done it and I've found out how wrong I was. I want you to know how much I appreciate your courteous, gentlemanly treatment. It stopped me from making a fool of myself."

The trooper glanced quickly at my license, which was in good order, and smiled back at me. "Where are you headed?" he asked me. I told him where I was going—I didn't make any excuses— and then waited for his next move. That summons still looked like a sure thing to me; frankly, I felt I had it coming. But, to my surprised delight, he said, "Well, take it a little easier from now on. I hope you get to your meeting on time. Good luck with your talk." Then he waved me on and I continued on my way. I got there in time and the speech went over fine.

Here was a perfect example of the power of on-the-spot ingenuity in making a favorable first impression. Result: he gave me a break. Whether he realized it or not, the trooper sensed my genuine and unexpected compliment, which automatically switched his thinking from writing a summons to patting his own ego on the back. Both of us came away from the episode feeling fine about the whole thing.

FIVE PRINCIPLES ON THE USE OF INGENUITY TO MAKE A GOOD FIRST IMPRESSION

1. Use the unexpected compliment.
2. Turn the spotlight into a personal theme. For example, talk to the gruff married salesclerk as though you believe she is single, and watch her pull out all the stops to serve you.
3. Assume the other person will react exactly opposite to the way he believes he should.
4. Say something that will surprise the other person, like highlighting an ability of his that you admit is superior to yours.
5. Avert a serious or pensive mood at all costs, especially by the interjection of humor. You can't beat appropriate humor when it comes to making a good impression or a good speech. Keep a notebook of special ingenuity-type anecdotes and review them periodically so that the key lines will remain fresh in your mind for split-second use.

SIX KEYS TO HELP YOU MAKE INVALUABLE FIRST IMPRESSIONS

Here are six keys that you can use to open the door to good first impressions, each illustrated by a true case history.

1. *Make the other person like you and become interested in you immediately.*

You cannot possibly use this key to advantage unless you put the spotlight on the other fellow instead of yourself. That is exactly what Harry did when he was faced with a difficult business situation. His problem was to tell an old friend and associate that he was going to promote a newcomer over him.

Harry did this by conditioning his friend's disposition. One by one he reviewed his friend's good points, the innumerable contributions he had made over the years to the benefit of

Harry's department, and his personal advancement. Not until Harry was sure that his friend saw eye-to-eye with him as to where he stood did he venture to introduce the candidate for the promotion he planned for him. And then Harry was careful to point out that the newcomer had special training and experience that qualified him for the job.

This was an effective practice of Harry's. He never believed in introducing someone to either good or bad news without first carefully laying a solid groundwork for the most favorable reaction to the news. As he told me once, "Unless you make sure by the proper introductory groundwork that a person likes you, you can thwart your objectives completely when you are faced with the task of relaying either good or bad news."

2. *Start the other person off on the right track by doing something or saying something that will put the spotlight on him at once. It is a little like writing the lead for a magazine article; you must get the reader deeply interested by the first paragraph.*

Take, for example, the case of the salesman who had succeeded after many months of patient effort in arranging for an appointment with the purchasing agent for a large corporation. This salesman, Henry, was sufficiently interested in preparing the atmosphere for his ultimate sales success with this purchasing agent to take the time to look up his future client. This small effort paid off handsomely for Henry because he discovered, in examining this man's biography in a reference book, that at one time he had been a Canadian Mounted Policeman.

With this background fact at the tip of his tongue, Henry approached the purchasing agent with far greater confidence than he would have without it. He had the cue to get their initial conversation off on a friendly, receptive, and persuasive basis. The purchasing agent, who had long since left the Canadian Mounties for the more lucrative career in which he was now engaged, was most favorably impressed by Henry's unexpected introductory conversational lead. It turned out that 90 per cent of the ensuing conversation had to do with how this purchasing agent had enjoyed his experience among the French Canadians in northern Quebec, and only 10 per cent had to do with the business at hand. The fact remained that Henry walked off with a very big order, and the simple cue which left a most favorable first impression in the mind of this purchasing agent deserved most of the credit. Henry has had numerous repeat orders from this gentleman and never has met any further difficulty in seeing him almost at will.

There is really no surer way of making favorable first impressions than by seeking out the innermost abilities or hidden treasures that the other fellow is least likely to think you know he possesses.

In my opinion, the top secret to success, popularity, and a greater sphere of influence among people is the application of a paraphrased version of the age old maxim, "Know thyself." My recommendation is "Know the other fellow!" Such information having been obtained, it is then necessary to time its introduction to the other person as early as possible in your first contact with him. Then you cannot help but make a good impression with him and win him to your side.

3. *Overcome any envy or jealousy that you may momentarily feel toward another person.*

For example, there is no time when the first impression you make is more important than when someone is suddenly picked out of the blue and appointed to a position to which you may have felt you were entitled. On this point it makes no difference whether you are a shoe clerk, a stenographer, a teller in a bank, the chief chemist of a plant, or the vice president of a corporation.

Take the case of Johnny D., a middle aged and quite successful department store manager. One day, quite unexpectedly, Johnny D. received a notice to the effect that his department store now had a new general manager. This was the position Johnny D. had been aiming for. It was quite a blow to him when he discovered that a dark horse had suddenly come out in front.

He had two courses of action open to him: (1) to pretend that he was happy about the new man's appointment and cover up his disappointment while he marked time in the hope that this newcomer might trip over himself, or (2) to set out immediately to make a favorable first impression on the new general manager, to back him up in the hope that he could help him become president. Fortunately for himself, he followed the latter procedure.

He arranged for an appointment with the general manager and he went to this appointment fully prepared. The general manager was deeply impressed, almost overwhelmed, when Johnny D. came into his office and systematically demonstrated his genuine interest in helping him tak .he next step up to presidency of the firm. Such a deliberate choice of the more positive action by Johnny D. paid dividends in time. About four years later, when Johnny D. became general manager and the man he succeeded assumed the presidency of the entire chain of department stores, Johnny D. knew how much his favorable first impression had worked in his favor.

In the course of my experiences, I have seen persons set up lifelong roadblocks for themselves by outward evidences of envy or jealousy. These emotions can ruin your future and stop you dead in your tracks unless you suppress them and in their place foster the right attitudes.

When a close friend wins an honor or a promotion, try being the first to extend your congratulations. He will never forget it and, if you knew the facts, you would be astounded at how few notes of congratulations such people receive.

Never complain or start rumors on the job when you learn that somebody has received a raise in salary and you were by-passed. Most supervisors are fair and honest when it comes to the handling of salary increases. You can always ask for an honest appraisal of your worth, of course, but never base such a request on the premise that you deserve a raise as much as "so-and-so."

Beware of belittling someone's personal abilities when you learn that he or his wife has suddenly inherited a large sum of money. I have seen tragic consequences as a result of a person spreading the word that "It is a good thing his rich uncle left him a small mint—he would never get that far on his own."

If the "big boss" decides to give a close relative of his a chance to prove himself in the company, then hold your tongue! Give the relative every chance to carry his own load himself. Let the "big boss" hear by the grapevine that you think he's playing favorites and you might as well forget about going any higher on the ladder yourself.

Suppress all expressions or comments that smack of envy or jealousy. They can easily become "nails" in your "coffin of failure," the kind of nails, alas, which sharpen rather than rust with age.

4. Try to talk in terms of the other fellow's interests or what he wants to hear.

It is the easiest thing in the world to steer any conversation; you can always control it if you really want to. As George L. told me once, "All that I know, and most of what I get paid for, I have gotten by making the other fellow talk to me about what interests him the most."

George is a fellow who has a lot of success behind him, too. It isn't at all surprising, though. He's the most popular fellow in any gathering a few minutes after it gets started, it seems. For example, I remember seeing him at work at a cocktail party in a Philadelphia Main Line home. He had never met the host (a prominent lawyer, well-known for his interests in and knowledge of early American history) before, but within five minutes after meeting him, George had captured his interest and attention. And he had done it so effectively that the host's wife repeatedly had to nudge her husband to show a little more courtesy to some of the guests who enjoyed much higher "social register" ratings than George.

How did George manage to capture the attention of this man so completely? Within minutes of meeting him, he struck up a conversation on a topic in which he knew his host was intensely interested. As a matter of fact, George went so far as to "bone up" on some of the less obvious technicalities of certain battles of the Civil War; in this way he could whet his host's interest in him by showing him he was not talking to an amateur. But George steered his host to the subject that was so close to his heart in a subtle manner. There was no element of "buttering up" in his bid for his host's attention.

The story about George points up your most valuable technique in steering conversations into channels of most interest to others and most value to you: take the time, go to the trouble to find out what your contact likes to talk about, familiarize yourself sufficiently with these topics so you can talk about them, and listen, in a truly receptive manner, to him talk about them.

Remember that whipping up harmonious conversational bonds is not unlike playing golf or tennis; unless your partner is good enough to give you a challenging game, you are apt to lose interest in him and the game very fast.

5. *Seek out, especially when you know in advance that you are to meet or associate with an important person, some hidden skill that few people know the person in question possesses. Then steer your conversation to bring this hidden skill out into the open. One way to do this is to ask a question that you are certain the other person would enjoy answering.*

A Dr. F. was the last person in the world that I thought would be a "fanatic" about magic. He was a world-renowned physicist who could give three-hour lectures on thermonuclear fusion processes!

We were at a summer conference midst the wonderful setting of Colby Junior College at New London, New Hampshire. A group of us was seated under the trees on a pleasant lecture-free afternoon and Dr. F. was with us. Unbeknown to most of us, Dr. F. frequently displayed his prowess at magic at charity benefits in and around his home town. One of my colleagues diverted the technical nature of our discussions to this "hidden" skill which Dr. F. had by asking him to tell us about some of the unpublicized feats in Houdini's lifetime. The result was a most fascinating afternoon for all of us. But of greater significance to my colleague who had asked this question was the fact that the following summer he was invited to present a technical paper on his research work at the conference. Such an invitation did much to raise the professional reputation of the young man in question. It was more than a coincidence that he had been extended the valued invitation by a program chairman who was, of course, Dr. F. himself.

Each of us enjoys taking the spotlight, especially when we can do it on familiar ground. Do your part to shine this spotlight on your friends now and then. Here are a few ways that I put this principle into practice:

Wilbur, a scientist I know, is also an expert magician, possessing an ability that people at a party enjoy. But they would not expect Wilbur to be a magician, and now and then I have, under appropriate circumstances, been able to get Wilbur to have a lot of fun displaying this talent.

Lou is an engineer who loves to cook. His own recipes are becoming increasingly appreciated and in demand. You should see his eyes light up when a group of lovely ladies suddenly surround him for recipes, after I have passed the word along to them.

Gene, a machinist, has a hot house and knows more about the names and life cycle of flowers and plants than most botany professors. I am constantly going to him for help and referring others to him for gardening advice, too.

6. Say something or do something that will help to make the other fellow feel superior to you at least in one particular way.

Mrs. N. was a lover of the classics. Before she got married she had been awarded a master's degree in Latin. Yet for years she stood alone in her household as the champion of Latin as a language that should be kept alive and taught more widely in our schools.

Her husband was a famous young scientist who had little time or interest in Latin; to him it was a dead subject that should be allowed to fade away with horses and trolley cars. But one day his indifference to Latin was promptly dispelled. A politician in the neighborhood stopped at Dr. N.'s home that day; he belonged to the "other" party. (Dr. N. had heard Mrs. N. speak quite uncompromisingly about this politician on many occasions, even though she had never met him.) He asked to see not Dr. N., but Mrs. N., for a purpose he made clear very promptly. He was working on an important political speech and wanted to use some Latin quotations in it. He had been told that Mrs. N. had a master's degree in Latin. Would she be so kind as to double-check the accuracy of the Latin quotations and their English equivalents?

The impact that this politician made by this first personal-contact impression still resounds in the "N" household. At voting time, to this day, Mrs. N. votes for one political party and Dr. N.

for another. Prior to this incident, they both voted, of course, for Dr. N.'s party.

You, too, can make good first impressions in life by going out of your way to make others feel superior in one way or another. Here are a few typical situations.

1. If you need a fast typing job, go to the stenographer you believe can do the fastest job for you and tell her why you decided to ask for her help.
2. See how favorably your wife will react when you ask her opinion of a business investment, because she has been so right in the past.
3. When you are in a cab, make a note of the driver's name on the card. Then develop the conversation on a theme suggestive of his background. For example, if his name obviously is Italian in origin, start talking to him about Italian opera or Italian artists, and, as his disposition improves, watch your ride get smoother!
4. Ask your boss for his confidential guidance on a personal problem because you have such a high regard for his valued judgment as demonstrated by his decisions on the job.

You don't have to limit your efforts to impressing people you are meeting for the first time. Even more valuable are the impressions you make on the people you meet every day, the people you live and work with year after year.

Still first impressions play a vital role in every walk of life. They can influence the tempo of the day; the one you make on your boss in the morning, on the children as they march off to school, on the breadman, the mailman or the laundryman. Take notice how that very first expression on your face or the expression on the other person's face literally determine the mood and the pleasure or displeasure that you, and he, receive out of your first daily contacts! In addition to having life-long impact on your success and popularity, first impressions also regulate your day-to-day, hour-to-hour pleasures and satisfactions.

In recapitulation, here are the six keys to making good first impressions. Learn them well and apply them when the appropriate situations arise:

1. Make the other person like you and become interested in you immediately.
2. Start the other person off on the right track by doing or saying something that will put the spotlight on him at once.
3. Overcome any envy or jealousy you may momentarily feel toward another person.
4. Try to talk in terms of the other fellow's interests or what he wants to hear.
5. Seek out some hidden skill few people know a certain person possesses and then steer the conversation to bring this hidden skill out into the open.
6. Say or do something that will make the other fellow feel superior to you at least momentarily in one particular way.

3.

How to Get Others to Do More Than You Expect Them to Do for You

---

I N THE COURSE OF MY STUDY OF THE MOST SUCCESS-
ful people I know, twelve clear-cut principles emerged that I
would like to detail for you. Each of these principles was useful
to these people to help them get others to do more for them than
they counted on! All of these successful people made their high
marks in life because they realized in time that a man seldom can
reach his goals by bread alone or by his own energy exclusively.
The more assistance you can obtain from and through others, the
higher will be your success grades.

TWELVE PILLARS TO BOLSTER THE OTHER FELLOW'S SUPPORT OF YOU

1. Do Things for People They Don't Expect

When it comes to getting others to go all-out for you, perhaps
there is no place like home to begin. For example, the next time
you get up to go to work in the morning, try awakening your
wife by patting her brow gently; then hold her robe for her as she

gets up to prepare your breakfast. See how effective this little consideration is in helping to get your day off to a good start.

Take time to praise that dimple, pretty nose, or nice figure your wife may have, when she least expects it, and watch how much more neatly pressed your shirts will be, or how your laundry will always be ready and waiting for you! Just as such little things will spark your wife or loved ones to do more for you, so also you can get associates, even strangers, to want to give you more than you can rightfully expect of them.

For a long time the girls on the stenographic staff of a Chicago firm were puzzled by the staunch devotion of a certain secretary, Mary B., toward her boss. It seems that Mary B. would do the unusual to please this man; she worked through coffee breaks, lunch, or even overtime, just to finish some typing job in which her boss was especially interested.

One day while visiting this man, I discovered the "magic wand" which he held over Mary B. It was simply that he showed her the utmost in gentlemanly attention and respect. There was something about the way he talked to Mary B.; his tone of voice, the little courtesies he expressed, his occasional off-the-cuff comment to visitors, as "wonderful secretary," "I don't know how I would get along without Mary," and so on, all of which kept his secretary in the most positive frame of mind. She wanted to feel she was standing back of him. She wanted to see him get ahead and did everything she could to help him.

The wonderment for Mary B.'s associates was her inside-out transformation. Prior to becoming secretary to my business friend, Mary had been assigned to a gruff, dictatorial department head. His lack of attention and appreciation had led Mary B. to two-time at every opportunity. She became a devoted, superconscientious secretary because her boss took the time to do little things to please her, to swell her pride in her job.

When I review persons who, like Mary, show extraordinary loyalty and devotion to their immediate "boss," I am struck by their record. In each case, they are responding to a basic principle: cooperation is the inevitable reward for consideration. You will find this truth invaluable to your success in life if you will only apply it.

Here are some suggestions you might put to work:

1. Go out of your way to ask your children to play with you, a game of badminton, checkers, or cards, and watch how refreshing their consideration for you will become. I recall one vacation with my family when I devoted more time than usual getting the children to play with me. Out of this came one of the most thrilling and spontaneous compliments I have ever received. My son, Bill, came over to where I was reading a book one evening and said, "Gee, dad, I really do like you!"

2. The next time your pastor delivers a short, soul-stirring sermon, send him a little note of thanks and stress how impressed you were by the short, straight-from-the-shoulder delivery. You will be doing much to spur him to repeat such a performance and thereby help him better serve his audience, especially those who find that long, dull sermons prevent them from getting as much out of their religious services as they should.

3. The next time you feel you must register a complaint with someone, try consideration first! For example, I remember when George bought a used car for his wife. Soon after it was delivered, they began to have all kinds of mechanical trouble with it. George called the head of the firm that sold it to him and said, "Mr. V., everything I have ever heard about your firm has led me to believe you stand behind each car you sell. I haven't the slightest doubt that you will fix up my wife's car to my satisfaction." George then listed the defects one by one. Mr. V. put one of his best mechanics on the job and George has been more than satisfied ever since. If he had "raised the roof" with Mr. V., the chances are he would have gotten some attention, all right. But the repairs would have been done half-heartedly, just well enough to keep the car functioning well until the 30-day guarantee ran out.

2. Never Let a Day Go By Without Making Several Compliments

I knew a man who claimed that he owed most of his success in life to a very simple formula that he followed. What was this formula? "For thirty years now," he told me, "ever since I took my first job in industry, I have never let a single day go by without making at least five deliberate compliments. Sometimes I have had to give them to members of my own family! Believe it or not I have discovered that my family and relatives are just as responsive to the magic of a compliment as are friends or total strangers."

Tomorrow, try this man's techniques of making compliments pay dividends. Here are some examples of how he handles situations in an average day:

1. He receives a telephone call for some guidance on a problem. Before hanging up, he says, "Bill, it always is a special pleasure to try to answer your questions. Do give me a chance to be of help again soon!"

2. The trash men happen to be picking up the trash as he comes home from the office. The previous week they had carried off what he thought was a small mountain of "junk" from a cellar-cleaning binge. He stops to talk to them just long enough to impress on them the vital importance their weekly pick-up to him in his efforts to keep his home and grounds in tip-top shape.

3. That evening his dentist finishes an inlay for him on a back molar. "Dr. K.," he tells him when the job is done, "you've done a terrific job for me on this one. I'm sorry I moved my mouth a bit when you took the first impression. But, believe me, I think the world of you for so painstakingly starting over from scratch to do the job right."

Therefore, to make the use of compliments most effective, it is necessary for you to:

1. Give compliments without expecting any in return.

2. Let the person who receives compliments enjoy them to the full; nothing saps the flavor from a compliment like giving one grudgingly.

3. Always keep your compliments on an individual basis so that a specific person is signalled out for them. A diluted compliment, like a diluted drink, doesn't carry much zip with it.

3. Show Others You Have Full Confidence in their Abilities

Not long ago I had occasion to engage the services of a plumber to do a rather expensive repair job in my home. I took the time to tell him how important it was to me to get the plumbing in first-class shape. (I can't stand showering with lukewarm water!) By telling this plumber that I was placing my full confidence in his judgment, and by giving him the complete responsibility for the job, I received an amazing response. Just by letting him know that I had full faith in his honesty and ability, I was able to get a job done at less than half the price, and with much better workmanship, than I would have had to pay otherwise. So often, if you will only open a person's mind to want to help you, or himself, you can do wonders for him as well as yourself.

Certainly such was the case when a new manager took over at our local supermarket. He replaced an elderly man who was of the old school, a man handling so much detail himself that he had his help confused and frustrated, causing his store to become a jumbled mess at peak buying periods.

The first thing the new manager did was delegate details. Each employee was given full responsibility to keep the stock in good supply in specific sections of the supermarket. Like magic, the grocery department acquired an orderly appearance; the produce department no longer looked as if a tornado had hit it; the shelves were always filled with what the customers were looking for. Because the new manager had clearly placed his complete trust in each member of his staff to carry the burden of periodically restacking fallen cans of groceries, half-mangled heads of lettuce, reshuffled cereal boxes, and so forth, they took pride and interest in seeing to it that such matters were always handled thoroughly. The last time I shopped at this store, the young man at the check-out counter told me he could not get over the complete change in work-atmosphere. "People don't scream anymore because they can't find what they're looking for, and our volume of business almost has doubled!"

If you are going to give anybody your vote of confidence, go all the way and you will be amazed at the extent of their abilities.

This principle has universal applicability; it is effective in solving all kinds of problem situations. For example, if your 12-year-old son asks to mow the lawn with a powermower for the first time, point out the precautions carefully, then leave him on his own, even if your wife peers nervously from behind a window curtain throughout the ordeal. Also, never ask an employee to do a job without implying that you want to hear about his problems only if he can't solve them himself.

4. Keep the Other Fellow's Enthusiasm Running High

"You can always contain and control the fire of enthusiasm," a boss I once had told me, "but if you ever put this fire out by throwing cold water on it you'll have a very hard time lighting it up again."

The least influential persons I know are those who are unable to generate enthusiasm in others; they are constantly spouting cold water! A leader in an organization who radiates a negative outlook on things can undermine morale and hold back progress more than a steep slump in the stock market.

Joe M. was anything but a "cold water" thrower. He could get as excited over another person telling him about an idea as anybody I've ever known. His specialty was, it seemed, that of pouring oil on the flames of other people's ideas and ambitions. As a result, there was a steady stream of people calling to see Joe in order to get their enthusiasm "recharged" just by being with him. Is it any wonder that Joe has recently been made the Director of Research for one of the largest chemical firms in Ohio? Even though he has long since forgotten some of the formulas from his college days, Joe M. couldn't help hitting the top job he has. His enthusiasm for sparking the enthusiasm of others was his ace quality. And his reputation and influence grew so well on the basis of it, that when the time came for the management to select a new research director, Joe M. stood out like a highway billboard.

Here are a few of the basic techniques for generating enthusiasm in others:

1. Repeat *their* ideas, not yours. For example, "Joe, your sug-

gestion hits me between the eyes. You've really got something."

2. Never throw cold water on a conversation; always preheat your negative position when it is necessary to take such a stand.

3. If you need financial backing, never seek a loan. Try to sell others an opportunity to invest some money instead.

4. When you find enthusiasm for a proposal waning, check your timing. That may be causing the chills. Retrench until the atmosphere is more responsive to your position. One man I know uses a stock phrase when he finds himself in an atmosphere of vanishing enthusiasm for his stand or proposal: "It suddenly occurs to me that this matter deserves to be slept on a couple of more nights."

5. Show Your Appreciation of Effort in Your Behalf

Of course there are more valuable things than money can buy! And most of them will not even cost you much in the way of effort.

The last time I had my regular physical examination, my physician showed me several beautifully autographed books by a prominent author. He explained to me that this author had injured his arm while ice skating and appeared at his residence at 10:30 one evening in intense pain and suffering some shock from the fracture. The author was taken to his home because it was nearest to the skating rink where the accident occured.

The physician did what he could to ease the author's pain, put on a splint, and gave him a sling. With that he never expected to see this patient again because as he lived some distance away and would go to his regular physician. But he did. As soon as the author recovered enough to do so, he paid a return visit to the physician who had befriended him. It was to re-express his appreciation and to leave with him autographed copies of each of the several very successful books he had written. I could tell from the satisfaction with which my physician told me this story (I'm sure he repeated it with equal enthusiasm to all his patients) that each of those books had more lasting value to him than checks worth many times their market value.

Harry gets along lovingly with his mother-in-law, and his marriage is a happy success. How does he do it? He shows his mother-in-law how much he appreciates her! I have, for example, heard him say to her, "When you taught your daughter how to sew long before I married her, you made it possible for us to have more money in the bank now," and, "Just how do you get such rich flavor into your Yankee pot roasts?"

Dr. R. is a prominent executive whose organization hums with an exciting *esprit de corps*. His appreciation for the people down the line is behind much of it. He is constantly writing notes by hand to department managers or department janitors in appreciation of something done beyond the call of duty. And, busy as he is, I have yet to learn when he has failed to stop by to tell someone how happy he was to learn they had a new baby or how sad he was to hear of a bereavement in a family. Such expressions of appreciation of fellow employees by a top executive may seem obvious. Yet so very rare in practice. Most executives deserve to be more popular than they are, but their aloofness shields their full personalities from their employees and also detracts seriously from their effectiveness. People on the job who are known as "good Joes" are, without exception, those who never miss an opportunity to show their appreciation to others who are doing things to help them on the road to success.

6. Admit Your Own Limitations without Losing Face

The use of the deft approach to getting your associates to do much more for you and your company is invaluable. One executive in particular comes to my mind. He was especially professional in the way in which he went about getting more out of others for his own advancement.

One day, faced with a very great problem, which necessitated skills in an area of production for which he had not been too well trained (he was a chemist and the problem at hand involved the crash construction of a new engineering pilot plant), this man called his staff together and said to them, "Gentlemen, I'm a chemist, not an engineer. We are faced with a difficult but pressing engineering problem. I don't know how to tell you in specific terms what to do, but I do know that you gentlemen can do it!"

Such humility on the part of a top brass who openly admits his limitations, and who doesn't hesitate to let the members of his staff know when they are better able to meet a specal task than he, is a mark of a great leader as well as a man who is headed for the very top.

Always remember that when you admit your own limitations others will grab the opportunity to fill the gap for you.

7. Go to Bat for the Other Fellow and Let Him Make Your Home Run

Many years ago I befriended a man who was a clerk in the storeroom of a manufacturing plant. He had been accused of stealing material from the storeroom. I knew the man and refused to believe that he would do such a thing. I went to bat for him. I succeeded in proving that the missing tools were stolen by a young employee who was a "hot rod" enthusiast wanting to use them on his car; the tools were "on loan," as he put it when the facts were brought to light. This man was vindicated and still has his job.

From that time forward, the storeroom clerk always tried to do "extra" little things for me. Few pleasures are more satisfying than those which come from asking a person to do something and seeing that person do it with both hands and his sleeves rolled up in a spirit of unleashed willingness.

Years later, when my friend learned that I had a son who had become an enthusiastic baseball fan, he handed me a package for my little boy. In it was a brand-new baseball personally autographed by Lew Burdette and three plaster miniatures showing two ball players arguing with a stone-faced umpire.

I know that my son will treasure these little statuettes as long as he lives. But what is equally important, I will never be able to pass his room and look at them without feeling a little warmth in my heart for someone who is dedicated to doing things for me.

The most glorious stories in American history are those in which the rights of a minority, or the "under dog," have been championed and upheld. This same doggedness to go to bat to prevent anyone from being tramped upon can be used by you to add stature to your reputation. One very popular and success-ful man I know applies this principle in his dealings with people in these ways:

1. When he hears a derogatory statement about somebody, he doesn't challenge it outright unless he has ample facts to squelch it. But what he always does as a matter of policy is to come forth immediately with a complimentary com-ment about the person being trodden upon. He argues that in this way he supplies ballast for the accused so that time is gained for the *facts* to come out in the open.

2. He refuses ever to permit a completely negative viewpoint to dominate a conversation, even if it only has to do with the weather.

3. Any time he learns that a person has made a mistake, es-pecially a serious mistake, he sets out immediately to do all he can to help that person admit and correct it. In one in-stance he helped a bank employee who had juggled his account square himself with the bank president without anybody else learning about it.

The merit of this important principle is that people always re-member and appreciate a person who offers a helping hand when they do not have a selfish motive behind it.

8. Recognize, Respect, and When Appropriate, Overlook the Other Man's Quirks and Whims

When it comes to understanding others and treating them in such a way that they will do more for you, it is necessary to ap-preciate that our society is made up mostly of persons who have their own idiosyncrasies. It is most important for a harmonious understanding of human relationships always to be aware of the fact that the other fellow should be allowed at least as many quirks and whims as you!

I have known some people who lost valuable opportunities to get ahead because they showed a peculiar sensitivity and irrita-tion toward others with whom they came in contact. For ex-ample, one chemist I knew could not stand his boss's pet habit of periodically sucking air through his front teeth while he talked. This chemist was so neurotic about this habit that he acted and became almost openly antagonistic towards his boss. Yet his boss was a good man who had the full interests of his associates at heart, a capable man well qualified and experienced in his job. The antagonism which this chemist developed, purely on the grounds of an individual's peculiarity, forced him eventually to transfer to a job where his future was much less promising. If he had remained where he was and overlooked the peculiarity of his boss, there was no doubt he would have advanced much faster and further. As it turned out, he lost the opportunity of a lifetime because he felt he was perfect and couldn't stand a minor and relatively trivial imperfection in the man to whom he reported.

Time and again you will discover that you can get others to do more for you by respecting their whims and tolerating their idiosyncrasies.

1. Whether in marriage or in the business world, try looking at others with half-shut eyes. You will be amazed at how appreciative they will be.

2. Never under any circumstances belabor another person's physical defect. You can make an enemy for life by making a joke out of someone's long nose, bald head, hairy chest, or bowed legs!

3. Search out your boss's whims and adhere to them. If he is touchy about late arrivals on the job or extra long coffee breaks, toe the line. You'll only spell failure for yourself by abusing his devotion to formal office hours in telling people he is an old fuss-budget.

9. Give the Other Fellow Credit, Especially When He Doesn't Expect It

Giving the other fellow credit for knowing something, doing something, or saying something for which he would least expect recognition is another way of winning more than the hoped-for support from other people. Tell a lawyer that he would make a great statesman and you surely will improve his performance in law! Show the other person how to like himself just a little more, and you will discover how easy it is for him to get to like you and thus boost you. But remember your fellow man has a built-in mechanism that somehow is capable of spotting insincerity as reflected in outward evidences of generous flattery. As one prominent executive told me, "When an associate pulls me aside, tells me he's my friend and there isn't anything he wouldn't do for me, a red light immediately flashes into my mind and I watch such a fellow as though he might be my worst enemy. My experience is that he usually turns out in the end to be just that!"

A good way to give the other fellow credit when he doesn't expect it is to use what I call the "repartee compliment." For example, when the bald barber comments on your full head of hair, you respond, "But, Joe, without the pampering you give it each time you cut it, I would look like a bushman."

When you give a neighbor a helping hand and he thanks you, you reply, "If there is one fellow I can count on when I'm in a pinch, I know it will be you, Harry."

When a business associate compliments you on the new suit you are wearing, you tell him, "Glad to know your tastes are so like mine."

When your boss gives you a raise and pats you on the back, it doesn't hurt to reply, "You deserve as much credit as I do, I could never do as good a job working under a different boss, I'm sure."

10. Build Up the Other Fellow's Self-Confidence

The most common and contagious malady in our work-a-day world is the lack of self-confidence from which so many persons suffer. Time and again I have seen individuals surge ahead as a result of one person saying or doing something to dispell another's lack of confidence and replace it with exuberance and a steady step or a steady voice.

A young scientist who once worked with me was to deliver a lecture based on some of his own research. It was the first time he was to give such a talk on his own. For weeks before the scheduled lecture I could sense how upset he was about it. He was worried about some of the authorities in the audience who might take issue with him and tear his interpretations to pieces.

One day I took him aside and, without making a special point of it, told him a story. "Bill," I said, "I thought you might enjoy hearing how I got my 'feet wet' when I gave my first science lecture. It was before an American Chemical Society meeting in Atlantic City. I was so nervous about it that my wife showed up at the lecture hall just in the nick of time, with my slides which I had forgotten in my hotel room!

"After I gave the lecture, I awaited with baited breath for reactions. And, sure enough, there was one, but only one. A college dean took vigorous objection to the title of my talk! I had used terminology that conflicted with a publication of his own relating to a similar problem. Guess what I did? I asked the dean to suggest an improvement to the title. He offered it. I publicly accepted it. Later, the paper was published using the dean's suggested improvement. Still later, I wrote the dean to tell him how much I appreciated the title improvement he had suggested. That dean is one of my staunchest scientific friends today."

Once, when I demonstrated to Bill that there is nothing to fear about giving a scientific lecture as long as you either agree with your critics or request their advice on the points to which they object, he became charged with an abundance of self-confidence. He now had the key to give him a logical exit from an embarrassing spot he might get into and his lecture was a big success. You should hear Bill deliver a scientific talk today!

A prominent scientist I know is a Milquetoast in his dealings with people because he lacks self-confidence; unless he can build himself a back door out of which he can slip, he refuses to express his honest opinion about something. This has been a serious handicap to him. He enjoys an excellent reputation among his conservative fellow scientists, but his lack of self-confidence has been responsible for him losing out on several promotions that would have brought him into top executive posts.

It is unfortunate that he didn't run into a boss who realized his weakness and then deliberately set about to build up self-confidence in him. In this way, the boss could have acquired for himself a first-rate technical assistant who was loaded with sound ideas for successful commercial development.

This is exactly what happened to Gerald, a development technician with a Midwestern plastic producer. Gerald was employed in the control laboratory doing simple analysis. His lack of self-confidence stemmed largely from the fact that he did not have a college degree. Yet his supervisor as well as others found that Gerald frequently offered excellent suggestions for solving production problems.

An opportunity came along; Gerald was offered a spot with great promise in the production department. He turned it down. He said he felt more secure in the analytical laboratory because he knew he could do well there without a college degree. He was unable to see how he could make out in production in competition with college-trained engineers.

)Gerald's supervisor reported this decision to his boss and it was then that steps were planned to bolster Gerald's self-confidence. Some days later, the plant manager handed Gerald a check for $250. It was in recognition of a suggestion of Gerald's, made weeks before, which had helped to increase the production of a certain type of film by ten percent.

The next thing the plant manager did was to talk with Gerald and tell him the company would pay tuition fees for him if he would take evening courses in engineering at the local university. Gerald now responded with interest.

Two years later, when Gerald was approached to take over as a production supervisor, he accepted and in doing so he found himself in his real element. His self-confidence had been built up so successfully by the patience and understanding of his supervisors that Gerald earned the production manager's spot in the due course of time. Today, he not only has many college graduates under him, but he also has an engineering degree. Furthermore, Gerald is a great proponent of the value of building up self-confidence in others. He is convinced that there is no better way to get others to provide for your own future success.

11. Never Be Satisfied with Giving only Average Service

Not long ago we became interested in the purchase of a new home. The first step was to select a reliable real estate firm. I contacted three of the most prominent real estate agencies in our community. In each case, one of their salesmen took me out to various homes that were up for sale. They gave me their sales pitch. After reviewing the statements and the stories of all three salesmen, it became very evident to me which of the three with whom I would do business.

The man I selected was George. The reason I chose George over Henry or Bill stemmed entirely from George's persistence to be of more than average service to me. He proved to me that he was interested in filling my needs first and collecting his commission second. As George showed me through each house, he came to know exactly what we were looking for. He did not hesitate to discourage certain houses that appeared attractive to me at first glance by pointing out specific disadvantages they might have to me as an author:

"(1) The den in this house is too close to the school playground. You would have trouble writing with dozens of children playing games within easy hearing distance. (2) Have you ever had experience with steel casement windows? If not, I do want to point out that this house is equipped with them. (3) The recreation room in this house could do nicely for your writing, but you might do better in a house with a less musty first floor den."

It became evident to me that in George I had a real estate agent who was giving my interests the highest priority. He was bending over backwards to be of service to me by telling me facts that he did not have to tell me. Both Henry and Bill were good salesmen; it could very well be that they were as honest and as truthful as George. But the fact remained that it was George's initiative to give me that "second undemanded mile" of service that caused my vote to be cast in his favor.

It was not until George showed me the fifth prospect that he tried to sell me. Then he said, "I believe I now have a clear picture of your needs. I think I can show you a piece of property that fills the bill for you." And it did.

In a salesman like George, we see the tremendous influence of doing all you can in the interests of the other fellow, even though it may appear like a temporary setback or loss for you. This is a far more valuable trait than back-slapping, story-telling, or any similar approach, in building up the kind of reputation that guarantees your steady upward climb.

People cannot help liking you, and wanting to carry your torch for you, when, as George, you provide them with much-better-than-average service.

At a luncheon date an editor told me that he always, with a pre-conditioned positive frame of mind towards him, looks for mail from a particular writer. This writer, he explained, stood out on his book because of his frank efforts to be especially helpful. Here are a few of the things which this writer did to give editors super-special service:

1. His manuscripts were letter-perfect, neat, and accompanied by a return fully-postaged and addressed envelope.
2. He always insisted that he was more interested in doing a good job for an editor than he was in picking up a check.
3. In some cases, he willingly did as many as four rewrites to insure meeting the editor's requirements. "If the job doesn't make you want to buy it enthusiastically, without any misgivings, please let me rework it for you until it does," was a common statement to editors by this writer.

The editor in question told me that he paid this writer high rates for material which may not have met as high a literary standard as that of other writers. "But," he said, "in the face of such energetic willingness to provide me with service, my opinion of this writer's work is bound to be somewhat inflated. Even so, all things considered, I would rather buy from him than from a competitor who is more worried about writers' rights and rates than he is in filling my bill."

There is no higher form of flattery than to have another person want earnestly to do a job outstandingly well for you. Develop a solid reputation for giving forth with superior effort and you will never be wanting for opportunities knocking on your door.

12. Ask the Other Man How He Would Solve Your Problem

By asking the right questions of others you can build up for yourself unbelievable treasures of information and wealth. Success does so often consist not in knowing the correct answers, but in knowing when and to whom to direct the proper questions.

Sit back sometimes and list the things you need to know more about; detail your areas of knowledge that you are weakest in. Beside each point list the person or persons that you believe could provide you with the needed information. Then proceed methodically to approach these persons either by correspondence or by direct personal contact to get your questions fully and authoritatively answered. You will be astounded at how willingly and freely some of the nation's foremost authorities will give you of their time and talent in return for the satisfaction that one good question from you can generate.

Mark was a businessman with a bent for things scientific. He was always intrigued by Einstein's Theory of Relativity, but he never did fully understand it. On his business stationery, he contacted a prominent physicist at Columbia University. He asked this learned and busy man if he would please give him his simplest explanation of Einstein's Theory just to relieve him of his repeated confusion over it.

Much to his pleasure and surprise, Mark got a two-page letter back from this physicist clearly explaining the Theory of Relativity once and for all. And the explanation was so easy to follow that Mark now is an "authority" on the matter—an accurate one, too—anytime this common subject arises at a luncheon, cocktail party, or similar occasion. This knowledge has helped Mark's prestige in no small measure in certain areas of his contacts.

Any time I have a difficult mathematical problem that is beyond my own depth, I head for a brilliant Chinese mathematician I know. Repeatedly he has straightened me out, or improved mathematical formulas in scientific papers I have had published. And he does so gladly because he loves mathematics and is delighted to help keep formulas in order when his help is asked.

In much the same way I have seen numerous successful persons unhesitatingly pave their way to the top with the aid of friends upon whom they know they can rely for answers in specific fields when they need them. The best things in your life are, indeed, free if you only are willing to give other people the pleasure of being asked good questions, those they can answer expertly! Here are a few additional illustrations of how this "pillar" has helped others to get more done for them:

1. A businessman received a telegram calling him to the bedside of his dying father. Time was of the essence! As he was examining plane and train schedules, a thought struck him: "Maybe Harry, the traffic manager in a large nearby corporation, could help me out." When he presented the problem to Harry, it was solved instantly because Harry knew the "ropes" as well as the right people to contact to get "Silver Desk" service. This man got to his father's bedside three hours before he died. If he had worked out his own travel schedule, he would have arrived twelve hours too late.

2. I know the president of one firm, with full knowledge of second and third-line supervision, who frequently asks clerks, secretaries, machine shop operators, and so down the line, to do special, personal favors for him in some area in which they are known to be proficient. By so doing he gets much more than his immediate personal problems (a grandfather's clock repaired, a package delivered close to a certain employee's home, a speaker for one of his community activities) solved. He builds up a corps of the most loyal supporters I have ever seen in any medium-sized business organization all along the line.

You never will be considered a bore if unhesitatingly you seek assistance from those who can help you the most. It is only when you take a superior stand that your popularity wanes. The world is filled with persons from corporation presidents to housemaids who are thirsty for the opportunity to solve your problems. In the end, your power to influence people and your success will depend on how effective a job you do in quenching this universal thirst among your associates, friends and acquaintances.

TWELVE PILLARS TO BOLSTER THE OTHER FELLOW'S SUPPORT OF YOU

1. Do things for people they don't expect and they will return the favor five-fold.

2. Never let a day go by without making several compliments.
3. Show the other person that you have full confidence in his abilities.
4. Keep the other fellow's enthusiasm running high.
5. Show your appreciation of effort in your behalf in a lasting manner.
6. Admit your own limitations without losing face.
7. Go to bat for the other fellow and let him make your home run.
8. Recognize, respect, and when appropriate, overlook the other man's quirks and whims.
9. Give the other fellow credit, especially when he doesn't expect it.
10. Build up the other fellow's self-confidence.
11. Never be satisfied with giving only average service.
12. Ask the other man how he would solve your problem and then stand back and let him.

4.

How to Put Human Nature on
Your Payroll

As soon as you put the other fellow's human nature "on your payroll," you have *two* persons, not just one, yourself, working to improve your paycheck, popularity, and success. By putting "human nature" to work for you, I mean simply the application of effective techniques which will spur others not only to do things for you, but to *want* to do things for you.

For example, let us assume you have as your objective reaching a job status two rungs up the ladder from where you now stand. You could, of course, do your job well and "let nature take its course." But your chances of achieving any objective in life are so much better when you follow a definite plan.

If you incorporate as part of your plan of advancement the stimulation and motivation of human nature in all those persons who might help you along the way, you not only will increase your chances of getting to where you want to go, but you will also speed yourself along the way twice as fast.

Drummond B. is one person I know who has most successfully capitalized on the support of human nature. Drummond literally soared past rungs on the ladder because of his ability to ride the waves of human nature. The first thing he did—something most of us all too often neglect—was to become as popular as possible with the "small fry," fellow workers at his own level. He did this by being nice to them, by helping them, by taking an interest in their personal life and problems. He made these people feel that they were important people in his life.

Having built himself a solid reputation with janitors, clerks, and secretaries by carefully working on the positive whims of human nature, Drummond raised his sights toward the next level. As every successful man will readily admit, nothing will give you confidence like knowing that the "little people" in any organization stand solidly behind you.

Drummond made it his business to be as nice and helpful as he could to supervisors throughout the organization. He knew that supervisors can often cast a deciding vote for or against a promotion from the ranks. This effort consisted in such actions as passing on rare stamps he happened upon to one supervisor whose son was an ardent stamp collector, discussing his hiking experiences with another supervisor, offering suggestions to another supervisor for improving the efficiency of his operations.

A step at a time, Drummond concentrated on winning the "confidence vote" of as many persons in his organization as he could. It is not by accident, to be sure, that he is today general manager of a multimillion-dollar Philadelphia corporation.

In order that you may better understand some of the motives and moods that steer or stimulate human nature in everyday life (they are points that Drummond B. had studied carefully), I have assembled a group of specific guiding principles for you.

BAROMETER OF HUMAN RELATIONS
Eight Typical Reactions of Human Nature

Here are eight typical examples of how human nature influences moods and motives in everyday life.

It is only human for:

1. Your boss to expect you to think the world of him.
2. A secretary to believe that she is the most dependable person in the office.

3. Your wife to believe that you think she is beautiful, and you are constantly wanting her to be with and near you.
4. Your children to sense your love for them.
5. The other fellow to be pleased with an audience (one person or a million) that shows it thinks the world of him.
6. A man with wavy hair to like a bald-headed man who sincerely says to him, "How I wish I had your head of hair!"
7. A person to react favorably to compliments or praise about his religion, political affiliation, or members of his immediate family.
8. A man who has a pimple on his nose to be more concerned about that than he is about many millions of people who are starving in Asia.

Putting human nature to work for you begins with an admission and recognition on your part of the other person's deep desire to have his own ego inflated. There is nothing sinister about this statement! It reflects as vital a drive in each human being as thirst for water. It is the golden thread which ties the Golden Rule together. There are dozens of situations in which you can benefit from showering human egos with thirst-quenching satisfactions.

GUIDE-POINTS FOR CULTIVATING HUMAN EGOS

1. Respect political and religious convictions, even support them if you can do so honestly.
2. Avoid getting entangled in any topics of conversation that might encourage you to take a blunt opposition stand.
3. Never top the other fellow's joke or statement of fact with a "better one."
4. Invite the other fellow to talk about himself, especially if you don't know him well or are making his acquaintance for the first time.

Each person, of course, will need a particular kind of ego-relationship. For example, conditioning your boss's ego is likely to require a different approach from that you would apply to your secretary or your wife.

Unhesitatingly prove to your boss or the person to whom you report that you will gladly take orders from him. You have to take these orders anyway if you are going to enjoy your work and get ahead. So why not use human nature, that of your boss's, to make the whole thing as pleasant as possible?

By showing your boss that you acknowledge him as such, you are more likely to find your pay-check growing more steadily and fatter, your title taking progressive steps up the prestige ladder. Your alternative is, of course, to stand still in your job, and gradually lose ground to competitors who are following a more effective program of putting their boss's human nature to work for them.

Henry is a good example of a person who knows how to put his boss's human nature to work for him. During the first three months with his first boss, he worked largely as a careful observer.

During this period, Henry's first responsibility was, of course, to demonstrate to his boss his loyalty, cooperation, and determination to do a good job. His sincere effort to avoid ruffling his boss's feathers was a secondary though important consideration. Henry might be accused by envious associates of "apple polishing" when in reality his actions were based entirely on the logic of common sense about human nature.

This was Henry's justification, for example, for actually making notes on the following subjects about his boss:

1. Likes and dislikes for jokes, music, sports, etc.
2. Best qualified areas of knowledge.
3. Pet expressions or habits.
4. Hobbies.
5. Political undertones.
6. Religious convictions.

Armed with such valuable "vital statistics" about his boss, Henry then stood a much better chance to avoid making that oft-times fatal slip which can prejudice human nature against you for life.

Henry's boss, it turned out, was very narrow in the matter of religious affiliations, so Henry simply avoided talking with him about religious questions. Instead, he encouraged his sensitive boss to elaborate on the seemingly vital importance of his hobby of stamp collecting. This was the last hobby in the world that Henry could get enthusiastic about, but it did wonders for his boss's disposition when he listened to him talk about it.

By encouraging his boss's personal interests, which his first calculated appraisal of him had revealed, Henry got his supervisor unconsciously thinking more highly of him in those technical areas where they shared responsibilities. Henry advanced each time his boss took a step forward. More importantly, he later moved into a top job in another division of the company when an opening arose. Henry got the nod only because his first boss had become so positively impressed by him that it was human nature for him to want to push Henry ahead.

Larry, on the other hand, constantly rubbed his boss's human nature the wrong way. He took the position that he didn't care what his boss thought. He was going to speak out, being the kind of short-minded individual who monotonously quips, "Well, it is a free country, isn't it?"

Larry would never hesitate to force his supervisor to speak out on subjects he didn't like to talk about. He took the common but so unpopular position that his birthright entitled him to resist any restrictions of his mental whims, boss or no boss. As a result, he kept falling flat on his face because it was only human nature for his boss to try to teach him a lesson now and then by tripping him in his tracks. Larry is still a technician and will always remain one until he realizes that when it comes to bosses or headwinds, you do best by "swimming with the current" or "bending with the wind."

Henry and Larry are two examples of how to and how not to impress your boss. But with your boss, or with your wife, on the job or off, the most respected conclusion is that in your dealings with people, if you want to influence and impress them, you have to swim with the current or bend with the whims of others. Your chances of winning supporters for your cause by bucking the stream of conformity, by striking out as an eccentric individualist, are slim. The reason for this is, of course, that the rugged individualist, the lone-wolfer, today has heavy odds against him. He would be unique if he could get to the top of the ladder without becoming a dictator, or by otherwise stepping on the toes of others and becoming generally obnoxious.

Human nature is what makes an enemy for life when you say a few words that are in the slightest way derogatory. Such words pick up momentum like an unleashed chain reaction. By the time they reach the person in question by the grapevine they have mushroomed into a devastating juggernaut intent on destroying you.

By the same token, when you deliberately, or otherwise, set free an extremely complimentary or praiseworthy story, opinion, or statement about somebody, and these get back to that person by the grapevine, with a credit line to you, you automatically make a friend for life.

I know one man who many years ago made a derogatory comment about a fellow chemist's technical ability and training. These few loose words have hurt him over the years a dozen times. As almost inevitably happens, his statement found its way back to the chemist in question. As a result the person whose ego had been hurt will probably capitalize on every opportunity to undermine the reputation of the person who "threw the first stone" at him.

Compare the seriousness of this negative verbal reverberation with Roger, the most popular fellow in the shop. What makes the difference? Word-wise Roger is the best reputation-bolsterer I have ever known. You will never catch him running down anybody's reputation; unless he can run with a reputation, he refuses to run against it, a policy that pays big dividends, indeed.

Words, like opportunities, seldom come back and if they do you are frequently helpless to do anything about them. So, beware! The pen may be mightier than the sword, but when it comes to being your own butcher, loose talk can be as destructive to you as a guillotine!

One man I know is a master of the art of making little diamonds out of almost every word he says. His name is Merrill, and the last I heard his title was that of executive vice-president. Here are a few of the notes I have kept about Merrill which, I believe, go a long way toward explaining his success with people:

Refrain from taking personal annoyance out on the other fellow. I have yet to hear Merrill say a cross word to anyone. Rather, when he is annoyed he usually says aloud, "Merrill, you ought to know enough to hold your tongue."

Notice the unusual, the trivial, the personal things. Merrill always begins his conversations with something about you, even if it is as trivial as commenting on a new tie or your cuff links.

Never criticize actions, only opinions. When Merrill criticizes anybody it is always about an action, never about an opinion— and then he invariably adds, "Of course, chances are I would have been even clumsier if faced with the same problem."

Make your "thank you" different, memorable. When Merrill thanks a person for a favor, it is seldom routine. Usually, it is something like, "You've been a wonderful host," or, "I feel that I've stepped up a notch in life for having met you."

Give a compliment wings. Merrill's art of making compliments is equally as subtle and powerful as his "thank you" comments. For example, on one occasion when he gave an employee a "Wise Owl" award for saving his eyesight by wearing safety glasses, I heard him say, "I know John's wife and children will be proud of him when he shows them this certificate." On another occasion, he patted an employee on the back with words when he said to him during a conference, "Bud, if more people could present their material as clearly as you just did, I am sure that conferences would become more valuable than management committees!"

If you wish to collect notes on the kind of words that can offend, all you have to do is listen to the remarks of the swarming hordes of humanity at the "bottom of the pile." Jack Z. is a good example of the type of person I mean. Here are the typical things —you ought to avoid such remarks at all cost—he says, which keep getting him in ever deeper trouble.

1. He cannot stand hearing a favorable remark about anybody without adding some detracting postscript like, "Yeah, but

he would not have gotten anywhere without the help of his uncle," or, "Maybe he is a hard worker, but he sure likes himself," or, "Anybody can get to the top if he uses his tactics."

2. He objects to new ideas on the grounds that they are not really new: "Jim thought of doing that years ago," or, "What's so new about that?" or, "The fellow who really deserved to get the patent is still a machine hand."

Notice how opposite Jack Z. is to Merrill. A person with Merrill's frame of mind and awareness of the importance of positive human relations would never react as Jack Z. does. Rather, he would be the first to say, "Wasn't his promotion wonderful, and so well deserved?" or, "I think he has one of the most inventive minds in the company."

If you wish to put human nature to work in your own behalf most obviously the thing for you to do is to see that only the nicest things get out of your mouth about what the other person says or does. Certainly it has been my experience that the most popular and successful people are constantly bubbling over with pats on the back for others whether they know them or not, and especially for those they want to impress or whose support they wish to gain. Also, it will always pay you to remember that most people take delight (many will vociferously deny this) in your quotations or opinions if they may in any way hurt you when broadcast. On the other hand, the nice things you say about people who will hear them eventually, at second or third hand, are your best goodwill ambassadors, your own public relations managers, and the best possible kind of advertising you can release in your own behalf.

How to Use Human Nature to Put Over a Speech

Let us suppose that you have been invited to give a talk before a Kiwanis Club. If you want your talk to be a big success, then you should plan on putting human nature to work right from the beginning. This means it will be far more important to the success of your talk to delve into the things of deep and personal interest to the people that you will meet at the luncheon. For instance, concentrate on asking questions and listening to the answers from the persons who may be sitting on either side of you long before you have to get on your feet and take the spotlight. Anything you might do or say to encourage a positive attitude toward you, by taking the time to listen to the people around you and to pry into their deepest drives and ambitions, will go far in setting the stage for a most successful talk later on. Give your audience the impression that you are going to be fully satisfied by occupying the floor for 15 or 20 minutes, that this amount of time in the spotlight will be more than ample to satisfy you. Prior to this, show your audience you are more interested in each of them individually than in yourself. Show them you are hungry to learn about them, and to listen to what they want to tell you.

The very best speakers I have known, the speakers who have impressed me the most, were those who made their audience feel very much appreciated for their attention, that their audience was doing them a favor to listen to them. Once again, such speakers knew how to put human nature to work for them.

There is nothing more deflating to an audience than to feel that they are simply robots who have to sit like school children and listen to an individual who has only himself in mind. Like the famous and very successful comedian, who at the end of each of his performances invariably thanked his audience not only in his own behalf but in behalf of his wife and seven children (he would name each one by one), it always is of the utmost importance to take leave of your audience on a note that will make them feel a little better for having had the patience to listen to you.

I could easily tell you of a hundred situations where showing an intense interest in the other fellow has helped me to get human nature on my side. Day in and day out a magic power within your easy reach is that released whenever you show real appreciation to somebody for his attention concerning any problems you might discuss with him.

ATTITUDE—THE PULSE OF HUMAN NATURE

Human nature, that of the other fellow, is extremely sensitive to your own attitude, expression, and even hidden thoughts.

Always avoid at all cost giving anybody a "brush-off," or "the routine treatment." Learn that the greatest power within your grasp over the other fellow is to discover what he wants to get out of you. More than anything else, give your undivided and sympathetic attention to his needs.

Take John T. His attitude literally draws people to him. He has a truly magnetic personality. Behind John, backing him up, is an attentive "open door" or "welcome mat" personality, a soft tone of voice and a well-measured rate of speech. He knows the effectiveness of treating the mailman or the bank president with the same unqualified attentiveness. I have seen John T. stop what he was doing, block his telephone calls, and give an old retired employee who stopped by to say "Hello" the fullest possible consideration.

The warmth and friendliness with which you project attitudes of calmness and genuine interest toward others are sometimes the barometers of your success in human relations: the extent of that warmth and friendliness determines the strength of people's similar response to you. When you rouse enthusiasm in the other fellow for himself, get him to feel that he is going to be a better person, or that your impression of him is about to move up another level on your chart, you win his human nature to your side because you convince him that you are working toward his interests.

Harold, a belligerent department head in a large manufacturing concern, was very hard to get along with. This man had been trained as an engineer. His promotions had come in rapid succession and he suddenly became responsible for certain operations that were not too familiar to him. He knew little about accounting, for example, even though he knew a lot about how to build a pilot plant. He was outright fearful of certain steps in the manufacturing process because the chemistry involved in these steps seemed so complicated to him.

At first, this manager had great difficulty in getting the cooperation of a particular subordinate, Bill. As a result, a personality conflict began developing. Fortunately, the subordinate in this case realized in time that he was going to get the wrong end of the stick if he pursued an antagonistic and uncooperative approach toward his boss. So Bill made a turn-about and decided to put human nature to work to rescue himself from a precarious situation.

The first thing Bill did was to set out as unnoticeably as possible to teach his boss confidence in a particular field in which he knew the latter was weak. Bill chose organic chemistry because he was best qualified in this subject. It had to do with the exact chemical reactions for making the plastic products for which Harold was responsible. Furthermore, he made a point of seeking Harold's help at every opportunity with engineering problems because engineering was a field in which Harold was outstanding.

Harold was pleased, actually astounded, at the way Bill was changing his overall estimation of him. Not only did he sense that Bill was cooperating with him, but he began acknowledging that Bill's guidance in connection with the chemistry of his manufacturing process was proving extremely valuable in terms of increased profits from his department's operation. And, just as Bill predicted, his boss gradually began giving him greater freedom of action along with increased responsibilities. A smooth working bond developed between them, and in place of the "chip-on-the-shoulder" response Bill once got from Harold, he soon felt the refreshing benefits of an almost paternal consideration from his boss. By taking the initiative, Bill had transformed an untenable working partnership into an harmonious give-and-take understanding on the job.

A housewife I know follows much the same strategy with her family. Time and again, for example, I have heard her say
To her husband:
"John, I'm really stumped for ideas on what to cook for dinner. Can you offer any suggestions?"
To her young son:
"Bill, mother is not quite sure how you would prefer to arrange the furniture in your room. How about telling me how you would like it."
To her daughter:

"Elizabeth Ann, I've been trying to figure out a new hair style for you now that you've grown out of pig-tails but it is not easy. I'll bet you've got some better ideas about a new hair-do for yourself than I have."

It Is Human Nature to Be Impressed by Noble Sentiments

Human nature is what permits you to get things done through people by appealing to their nobler motives. If you tell a man you are sure his wife would love to see a play for which you are selling tickets, you are more likely to sell him tickets than if you simply hinted to him that he himself would enjoy the play.

Time and time again, appealing to the more noble of men's sentiments will put human nature to work for you with the greatest of ease. Ask a man, no matter what his position may be, how his son or daughter is doing at college and you automatically pave the way toward his open-minded reception and acceptance. When you request his support or seek his backing, such a person is not likely to be found wanting.

Finding the sensitive spot in the other fellow's human nature can be one of the most valuable discoveries in your life. It can be as useful to you as a college degree and as valuable to you at times as having married the boss's daughter if you're a man, or his son, if you're a woman!

Eight Keys to the Sparking of Noble Sentiments in Others

1. Never ask a person to "do" something for you; always ask for "help."
2. Never ask for "money"; ask for "support" of a cause.
3. Never tell a child he or she "can't" do something; say they would make you very happy if they didn't do it!
4. Never tell your boss you deserve a raise; ask him if, in *his* opinion, your performance now seems to measure up to one.
5. Never approach a sales clerk with a "you-must-wait-on-me-immediately" attitude; always take the "I'm-sure-you-can-help-me-with-my-problem" approach.

6. Never tell the gas station attendant, "You do a terrible job of cleaning my windshield." See how clean he will get it for you if you tell him, "I come here for gas because you people do such a thorough job of cleaning my windshield."
7. Never tell your mother-in-law that she should "Keep your nose out of my business." See what happens when you say to her, "I can't understand the origin of all these mother-in-law jokes. You certainly go out of your way never to interfere with our private and personal business."
8. Never begin any conversation with, "The world is in a mess, isn't it?" Rather see what happens when you use, "Don't you think by putting our heads together we could eliminate some of the unnecessary misery in the world?"

If you ever must wax sentimental, be noble about it! You can increase your ability to influence and sway people by assuming they would rather be noble than ignoble. This is especially true of the "bully," or the chip-on-his-shoulder type of person. Notice how the most effective sermons are those which show you the way toward becoming a nobler person. The nobleman of past centuries earned their coveted reputations by exercising the kind of courage that made others wish they could be like them. Never miss an opportunity to help another person bring the warmth, so often shielded by a cold, mean, or unpleasant shell, out to the wide-open surface. People will love you, and bless your name, for helping them to do what their heart or conscience constantly tells them they should do, but don't because something about their personality or environment holds them back. So many of us need but a gentle boost to become better-living human beings, and we certainly would be forever thankful to those who might give us such help: the nobler the resulting behavior, the deeper the appreciation.

There is no better place to put the other fellow than on your own "payroll." To do this you must learn to anticipate the reactions of persons, and condition them in advance, so that they will always maintain a positive attitude towards you.

This means using words as salves, not swords, and never letting anyone feel you are giving him the "routine" treatment. It means, too, that you must always give the other fellow the chance to *express* rather than *suppress* his noblest sentiments. You can readily do this by applying one or all eight keys listed in this chapter.

5.

The Power of Persuasion: Life's Best Lubricant

O NE OF THE SURE SIGNS OF ABILITY IN A PERSON is his practice of peaceful persuasion to get what he wants done. The man who resorts either to verbal or physical force seldom, if ever, succeeds in getting anywhere. He may get what he wants, but he doesn't become very effective or generate much influence in his future dealings with people. On the other hand, the parent, the school teacher, the business executive, the clergymen, anyone who masters the technique of friendly persuasion, invariably succeeds in winning the other fellow's good will and strong support.

A popular song had as its theme for winning a maiden's hand and heart the two words "friendly persuasion." The use of friendly persuasion has a much wider value to you than just for winning your sweetheart's love. It has tremendous value in human relations and is a basic pillar upon which to build for yourself outstanding success with people.

I like to refer to the art of friendly persuasion as a method of applying "Life's Best Lubricant" to human emotions. Once you begin using this principle in your dealings with people you will soon come to realize that it is a magic means of fighting friction on the human scene.

Have you ever been bothered by a squeaky hinge on a door, a stuck nut on a bolt, or a rusty Stillson wrench? And perhaps after days or weeks of procrastination, you finally apply a drop or two of oil and suddenly the squeak disappears from the hinge, the nut comes loose on the bolt, and the wrench can be adjusted with ease.

"Friendly persuasion" can fight friction between people as effectively as oil can dispel friction between metals. Let me illustrate by some practical everyday examples how it can serve you as "Life's Best Lubricant" and thereby add real distinction to the success with which you are able to deal with people.

Suppose you have the problem of getting a youngster, who is very weak at arithmetic, to improve his interest in and his performance with the subject. Some parents might rant on, telling their child that without a sound mathematical background his future will be bleak. They may threaten him, and deprive him of treats or privileges. In the long run, however, the use of such forceful tactics seldom succeeds in making the youngster a genius at mathematics. The more you use force, the more he hates the subject.

Compare this approach with a parent I knew who was faced with this problem. This youngster, Johnny, was a bright boy in sixth grade. Yet each week he obtained below-passing marks. So this parent decided to prove to himself that Johnny did not lack ability. He was missing out because of attitude rather than aptitude, because of a lack of interest rather than a lack of know-power.

He did not scold his boy about his poor marks. Rather, one evening he said, "Johnny, I want you to let me help you with your arithmetic. The fact of the matter is I want to brush up on this subject myself, and I believe by doing some of it with you I can learn many of the simple rules of arithmetic that I have long since forgotten."

The first evening that this man worked with his son at arithmetic he discovered the essence of the youngster's poor marks. First off, he could see that Johnny did not yet have a spontaneous liking for the subject. He didn't really get enthusiastic about it. As a result, Johnny would read the arithmetic problems carelessly; he would interpret the question incorrectly and almost invariably get a wrong answer.

Johnny's father spotted this weakness and immediately began to persuade him to correct it. For example, he would say, "You know, Johnny, my biggest difficulty with an arithmetic problem —they are all really very simple—is that I fail to read the question carefully. Follow what I am doing and you will see what I mean. I am going to read each question carefully three times before I make up my mind how I am going to solve it. In other words, I want to teach myself first to understand clearly what the problem is before I attempt to figure out how I am going to solve it."

Ten days later both Johnny and his father were routinely looking each question over with a fine-tooth comb to pinpoint the problem. Then they would carefully figure out the steps required to solve it. When Johnny had his final mid-term examinations, he announced at the dinner table that the examination was a cinch! "You know, dad," he said, "arithmetic is really easy if you take the time to read the problem a couple of times so that you will know the right way to solve it!"

John's father was overjoyed. His son put his own point across for him! It was no surprise later when this parent received a note from Johnny's teacher telling him she was completely baffled by his son's sudden rise to the top of his class at arithmetic.

This very elementary logic, this disarming but effective use of the art of persuasion by Johnny's father, if applied throughout our adult lives to most of the problems of human relations we encounter, could make life much easier, more pleasant, and certainly more successful for all of us.

The effectiveness of friendly persuasion is universal, as oil is for fighting friction. For example, with divorces reaching staggering numbers, we can be sure that husband-and-wife relationships in our age are in urgent need of lubrication. So frequently, tragically, the drop of "oil," the recourse to friendly persuasion to smooth over ruffled feelings, comes too late to save the day or the marriage. The ensuing unnecessary heartbreaks and heartaches are among the unsung and unwritten blights of our modern times.

Judging from the tremendous number of words that are written on the subject, I think we can say that most men have some difficulty in getting their wives to see things their way. I am convinced that the reason for this is that husbands are apt to forget that the first step to open their wives' minds to their way of thinking is to prepare a favorable foundation for agreement!

Andy, for example, always complained to me that his wife, Ruth, was uncooperative and uninterested. She seemed to fight his every suggestion. What Andy failed to appreciate was that he also invariably took a negative attitude toward Ruth. He treated her as though she did not have a brain in her head! He constantly felt that she was not doing her best with the housekeeping and with her meal-making. Ruth could detect this negative shadow in Andy's personality and it rubbed her subconsciousness the wrong way. The result was frequent bickering and much ill-feeling, sometimes suppressed, but always there, smoldering beneath the surface. Neither Andy nor Ruth was making a very good success out of their relationship. These two fine people were missing out on happiness and contentment in their marriage.

One day Andy read a little quotation attributed to Billy Sunday. "Try praising your wife, at least once a day, even if it astonishes her at first!" Taking his cue from this sensible advice, Andy began to cultivate a persuasive, more agreeable attitude toward Ruth. When he greeted his wife now, there was always some compliment about the way she looked. When guests were dining with them, Andy always made a point of commenting at appropriate times, "Nobody makes sauce like my Ruth does!" Or, "I just can't get over that lovely suit Ruth made."

Similarly, Andy now began to tell Ruth that he knew how hard a day she must put in and that keeping the house shipshape didn't leave much room for her to take in some of those good daytime television programs! The fact of the matter was that Ruth did spend too much time watching television. She did throw meals together. She did not bring out the best in her figure! It was not until after Andy told her that he thought she was not doing these things that Ruth persuaded herself to bring them under control.

With marital problems, when two persons are brought into proximity and little squeaks of friction can sometimes develop into roars of dissention, the persuasive approach is all-important. Your chances of success in dealing with other people are seriously handicapped unless you are first successful at home base. The man or woman who has a burning desire to get to the top must first succeed in keeping the home fires burning happily and noiselessly.

SET THE OTHER FELLOW'S STANDARDS HIGHER THAN HE KNOWS THEY ARE

To make it as easy as possible for the other person to blow his horn for you, it is of the utmost importance to treat him as though he already is measuring up to—even beyond—what you expect or believe he is capable. There is no more forceful form of persuasion than setting a publicly acknowledged standard or code of ethics for the other fellow.

Yes, all through life, it is the same simple story. Nothing will make a person live up to an ideal like telling others in his presence that you believe he already is measuring up to that ideal. Give others the benefit of the doubt; always give them the positive side of the doubt and you'll be astonished by the amount of confidence they will give you. There are few more certain ways to make others want to do what you hope they will do to back you up, when you may have to count on them most.

Early in my career, I was in my boss' office when an urgent request came in for help from one of the company's plant managers. As I sat there listening to the conversation, I was deeply moved to hear the boss say: "Don't worry, Wood. I'll send Battista down to help you out. I know he can solve your problem faster than anybody else on my staff."

The fact was that the problem my boss described to me had little to do with the field in which I was considered to be a specialist. Nevertheless, I loved the challenge the boss had so subtly placed before me. I showed up at the plant the following day, as promised. But I had spent three hours the previous evening studying information relating to the plant problem before tackling it; I felt that I could not fail the trust and confidence my boss had so unhesitatingly placed in me. And, as it turned out, we were able to solve the problem in record time and save the company thousands of dollars.

WHEN YOU USE FORCE, YOU HAMMER
AWAY AT YOURSELF

Each time you try to force a person to accept or acknowledge your point of view, you are driving a nail into the coffin for your future. You cannot force the other person to your way of thinking without his consent. The best way to obtain that consent and approval is to reach a common ground of agreement and mutual satisfaction. Otherwise, the penalty for forcing the other person to accept your part of the argument or your point of view is frequently serious. Usually the reaction has a delayed rebound, one that will hit you when you least expect it, sometimes many years later.

One day at a conference, Dick, the boss, lost his patience and sat heavily on Charlie, who kept insisting that his idea would save the company a lot of money. It involved a new assembly line scheme for putting a portable transistor radio together. Dick bellowed, "I'm boss here, Charlie, and I say the present assembly sequence stands."

Charlie was hurt, but he knew his idea was better; he refused to give up even though Dick had sat on him. Some days later, Charlie had a chat with his boss: "Dick," he told him in a friendly tone, "I know you always get behind a good idea once you are sold on it. Maybe I was over-enthusiastic at the meeting the other day about my assembly line plan, but I do wish you would give it another review with me. Maybe you would even be willing to try it out on the plant manager and get his opinion?"

This time, Charlie's approach worked. By making it easy for Dick to go over the idea with the plant manager, he had persuaded Dick's mind to unlock. The plant manager liked the scheme and told Dick to try it out on a small scale. It worked most efficiently and the estimators projected a saving of thousands of dollars.

This plan eventually not only netted Charlie a sizeable cash bonus, but helped Dick's stock with the plant manager, too. Today, pity the person who says or insinuates the slightest thing about Charlie. In Dick, Charlie won a lifelong friend and champion, a man who will no doubt do everything he can to push Charlie along to success.

Imagine how completely different things would have turned out for Charlie if he went around deprecating Dick's original dressing down to him, and later deliberately "squealed" on Dick, when he had a chance, to Dick's boss. Both men would have become embittered towards each other, and by the same token their progress to further success would have stopped dead in its track.

Charlie intuitively pursued the friendly persuasion approach at its "professional" best.

Because man is an egotistical creature, he reacts like the recoil of a gun. When anyone pushes something down a person's throat, when the human ego is trampled upon, he may temporarily acquiesce to save face. But the hurt subconsciousness probably always will be sensitive, abiding its time until an opportunity comes along that allows for a rebound, a chance to get even with the person who damaged or bruised the ego originally.

Such reactions are not always self-evident. If the truth were known, even in a great many cases where it appears that the person is literally turning the other cheek, the counter-reaction is seething underneath. The chances are that if and when an opportunity arose to slap back at the cheek of the person who struck first, nine out of ten times that opportunity would be used.

Help the other fellow to be right, prove that he is right, and you immediately put into your hand a key that will open up his mind toward you. There is no better way to get your point across than by helping the other person to want to agree with you.

One man I knew was an army major. During his transition to civilian life, he was extremely difficult to get along with. It turned out that he lived and worked on the principle of saying, "No!" to everything that came up right at the onset. Then, if he should change his mind later to "Yes," he thought he was being friendly and thus making a friend!

Of course, the contrary was true. Even though he would frequently reverse his initial decisions, the fact remained that his abruptness, his refusal to reach or even entertain a basis for initial agreement meant that he built up around himself a tremendous army of persons who disliked him.

The Persuasiveness of the Understatement

I found that the secret of putting my points across with this man was to go overboard in understating my needs, my wishes, or my requests for his services. It amazed me to discover what an entirely different person I was dealing with, what a co-operative and conscientious supporter of my own interests I encountered by playing things down with this gentleman.

For example, as a business manager, this man was responsible for secretarial help. Previously, when a department head's secretary was out ill for a week and he would request a substitute of the business manager, he invariably got the stock reply, "No! You will have to make out as best you can."

His negative outlook was such that he refused to let people tell him what they needed even though their needs were entirely legitimate. But look at what happened when I discovered how to put my point across with him. I phoned him and said, "I am loaded with work and my secretary will be out for a week. I think we can make out, if only you could arrange for someone to be at the secretarial desk to answer the telephone between nine and ten each morning." This meagre request received an unusually enthusiastic response. Like magic, a secretary would show up and she would be at the desk not only from nine to ten each morning but throughout the day! Furthermore, she managed to handle all of the regular secretarial duties.

There are many people in life like this ex-major who respond to a toned-down approach. It is important that you spot such persons in your life and work with them in this way. You will be unsuccessful in getting them to do what you want them to do if you approach them with the enthusiastic over-statement attitude; the way to such people lies in the persuasiveness of the understatement.

The technique and value of the understatement parallels the strategy of the person who, as Pasteur did, tries to prove he is wrong, not right. If your arguments are unsuccessful in proving yourself wrong, the other fellow can more easily recognize why you are right. Similarly, if by understanding your position you make it increasingly evident to the other person that you deserve greater credit, he will be driven in conscience to bolster the facts in your behalf.

The use of the understatement is bound to increase your ability to influence people for many reasons. Perhaps the most important reason is that it is the exception; the world is filled with exaggerating bores! Then, too, the understatement gives you the temporary advantage of being the "under dog," and it is a basic tenet of human nature to want to help the underdog, to improve his status.

Read carefully the annual statements by some of America's foremost corporation presidents. In all those cases where I have been close to the facts, I have been amazed at how carefully these successful men word their statements. Even when they knew they had new products capable of swelling their company's profits they invariably spoke cautiously and extra-conservatively about them.

Indeed, corporation presidents have been through the fire! They know all too well that a cautious understatement to stockholders, followed by a year of outstanding new profits, will do more for their security, their paycheck, and their long-term prestige than any other device at their beckon.

Still another way of persuading the other person to agree with you or to do something for you is to highlight exactly what benefits he will derive if he does what you hope he will do.

When you hail a cab-driver and ask him to take you into untraveled territory, for example, a suburban area, you will be amazed at his reaction if, on getting in the cab, you tell him that you can direct him to a spot in the area where he is almost certain to pick up a fare back into the city. I know, for I have used this technique frequently out of the Philadelphia International Airport. Most of the cab-drivers would prefer to shuttle back and forth to the center of Philadelphia where they can make more money than they would by going into the suburbs where it is all residential and unlikely that they can pick up a return fare.

When I order steaks from my butcher, I am certain to get an excellent cut if I ask him, "Did Mr. Brown come in to see you about some steaks? I told him to do so last week when he said he was looking for a good butcher to keep him stocked." Once again, the point being made is that the butcher who serves me does so more conscientiously because he wants to qualify for more of my customer-recommendations. I cannot recall when our steaks have ever been anything but the best!

Serve up a benefit to the other fellow on a silver platter and you invite him to do more and better things to improve your over-all status in life.

A supervisor who spells out the benefits his entire staff will reap if they work with him to reach a certain production quality or quota is bound to go farther than one who is intent on harvesting as much merit as he can only for himself.

Politicians are experts at applying this principle, especially in pre-election campaigns. Such orators are constantly promising benefits to each voter if he is elected. They know it is what they promise to do to benefit each voter that determines their popularity and likelihood of being elected. And, in everyday business life, as with political fortunes, the sincerity and the follow-through with which a person stands back of the benefits he holds out to others determines his ultimate success or failure in handling people.

HOW SUBTLE PERSUASION CAN SPARK
INTENSE INTERESTS

Shortly after I was married, I found that my wife had only a mild interest in my work as an author. An author can easily spend more time at his typewriter than a physician does at the hospital and on his rounds. It is easy for a wife to develop a subconscious jealousy of her husband's work, especially when she feels his devotion to his work is robbing her of his time and attention.

Realizing my problem, I went to work to put my point across to my wife, that through my work I was building up security for the entire family.

When we had friends in for an evening, I took the initiative to boast about the things that I wanted and hoped my wife would do voluntarily with me. For example I would say, "Helen is an indispensable partner. At the end of each month, she squares the bills away and settles all of the outstanding financial matters so that I don't even have to think about them."

On another occasion I would say, "Helen is essential to my writing success. She is an excellent typist, almost perfect, when she types my manuscripts. Her formal education in Latin helps in adjusting sentence structures, helps no end in polishing up my informal background in English composition."

On still another occasion, I would bring out clearly that I believed sincerely that Helen had great literary ability and that I knew that she would someday put it to good use. And she did, too, for she has sold articles to the *Saturday Evening Post*.

As I started to use the persuasive approach with my new bride, deliberate as it was, Mrs. Battista gradually developed an intense interest in handling the business end of my writing, in typing my books, and in writing fiction herself.

Dick, the son of a well-to-do executive, was employed as a routine copy man in a large New York advertising firm. For months, Dick's boss mulled over a method whereby he could get him to use his latent ability as an artist.

He had spotted Dick's flair for sketching, and, being a good boss who tries to bring the best out in those for whom he is responsible, he wanted to put Dick on a track on which he could go far, much farther, entirely on his own. But, since Dick had always had things so easy, he was in a rut. His salary, relatively meagre as it was, still provided him with adequate means.

One day Dick's boss had a talk with him and asked him if he would do a special favor for him. He gave Dick ten original gags and then requested that he draw them up for him, on his own time. A few days later, Dick left ten cartoons on his boss's desk. His boss told him they were well done and exactly what he wanted.

The next thing Dick's boss did was get in touch with a prominent literary agent he knew, and, after inserting Dick's by-line on the cartoons, he asked the literary agent to try them out in the better markets. Within ten days, Dick's boss had good news from the literary agent. *Look* had picked up one of Dick's cartoons, and *The Saturday Evening Post* paid on the line for two!

At this point, with a check for $240 on hand, Dick's boss called him into the office. He explained what he had done, and handed over the check to Dick.

The return for his effort was very impressive to Dick, and his appreciation for the trouble to which his boss went to point out the benefits of such an effort to him did the trick. Within six months, Dick was doing some of the best sketches for this advertising firm as well as selling an occasional new cartoon to the top markets. Dick and his boss became more than loyal friends. They are now two of six partners who own this Madison Avenue gold mine!

There is more to this story than Dick's success. Needless to say, Dick has been a constant booster of his former boss, and he always will be. More importantly, perhaps, his former boss also helped himself immeasurably. By spotting Dick's abilities and by realizing what they could do for his own company, he diverted excellent talents to ends which eventually helped his firm to obtain several huge accounts.

You have in the magic of persuasiveness what you might look upon as a foolproof law for getting others behind you. If you will learn always to give the other person more credit than he knows he deserves, he is always going to make an effort to measure up to the standards that you set for him; you will automatically persuade him to raise his own sights. Too many people accentuate the minimum when they should be boasting and publicizing the maximum about those with whom they come into contact. If you will give, give more than you get from the other fellow, for then he will carry you forward on his shoulders and be one of the most effective sponsors for your success and achievement.

Indeed, "friendly persuasion" is valuable in fields that extend far beyond that of courting a woman's love. It is the master key in getting people to like you, in increasing your popularity, and steadying your ability to influence and lead people. Without its day-to-day application in your own particular circumstances, you will have a most difficult time trying to become a really successful person at the art of dealing with others.

Most of the people with whom you will come into contact tomorrow will have one common thirst, your acknowledgement that they are right about something. You will be giving a new spurt to their life and improving your own chances of success by saying or doing things that will help to quench their very real thirst for a feeling of importance.

Help the other fellow to see the best qualities within himself, and you will transform him into your best asset. Treat the other person as the most honorable person you know, accept him as he is, let him know that you are proud of him, and you will be astounded at how liberal he will be in doing what he can to make your dreams come true. Here is the time-tested formula for winning all the support, cooperation, and influence that you will ever need to reach whatever goals you may set up for yourself.

Few people I know are more skilled at doing this than Stanley. Here are several of the ways in which he dignifies other individuals:

1. He thrives on trying to prove to others that they are right about various subjects.
2. Stanley never has an appointment with any employee, if he can help it, without first getting a few ego-statistics about him through his secretary or the personnel department. If he has to be firm with John or Tom about anything, it helps Stanley a great deal if he can lead up to this by spending a minute or two discussing the new baby in the family by name or how well a youngster is doing in high school.
3. He never compares one person's performance with another's. Rather, he always compares that person's performance today with what he thought it was six months or a year ago. What a difference this makes as far as Stanley's power to influence others is concerned!

Friendly persuasion is life's best lubricant for smooth and successful human relations. Force, firmness, or bluntness, on the other hand, will only push your reputation and influence down to the bottom of the pile.

The magic power of the understatement is unbeatable in winning positive support from the other fellow. There is no surer way to make him see how he will benefit from anything he might do to help you.

Always prove the other fellow is right about something, even about predicting last week's weather!

Keep yourself well-armed with ego-statistics about your day-to-day contacts.

Never make comparisons between persons; there is always the safer way of showing a person how much better he is doing today than he was a year ago. In this way you can make a person satisfied with himself and happy with you much more easily than you can by stacking him up beside a competitor in his own field.

6.

Make People Feel Important and
They'll Help You to Greater Success

EVEN THOUGH I HAVE NOT HAD THE PLEASURE OF
meeting you personally, there is one thing about you that I can
discuss and know with full confidence that it will interest you;
you, like all your fellow human beings, no matter who they are or
what they do, are most anxious to *deserve* a feeling of importance
in the eyes of others.

This almost insatiable thirst for importance can be a source of
great energy to you, a well from which you can draw a steady
supply of fuel for action, a current along which you can ride to
greater influence and achievement. "The desire to feel important
to only one other person," says my friend Dr. Roland Wright, "or
to two billion people is as much a part of man as his pulse or his
brain." In this chapter, I want to show you step-by-step how you
can use this universal thirst of human beings, this valid, oft-
proven sociological principle, to improve not only your lot in life,
but your stature and prestige in society as a whole.

But, first, let us examine your conscience and in all frankness
ask you to own up to motives that artificial social customs and
traditions have so devastatingly managed to suppress in people.

72

It does not require any power of mental telepathy or extrasensory insight to tell you that, as a normal human being, you are interested in making a hit with people; you want to be liked and respected, and you want to feel important. You want to feel that you are making a mark in the world, that other people look up to you as someone who has done something special to add to their life.

The full weight of historical evidence, of human biographies, and of modern psychological science tells me that you have the same deep drives, the same desires as everyone else, whether or not you realize or admit it.

Since this is now as universally a proven truth as Newton's law of gravity, why don't you do something with this "law of human nature"? Why don't you use this basic human drive in your daily relationships with other people? Why not learn how to satisfy this desire that all men have, so that you will not thwart your own desires by rubbing others the wrong way, by making them feel unimportant, and turning them against you? Once you know how to act with people so that their longing for importance is satisfied, you will find your own importance going up tremendously, and you will become an important person yourself!

The driving power in the work-a-day life of millions of us, the "oomph" that makes life more challenging and more pleasurable, is tied in with this principle of "importance" in human behavior. Things people do or say to you can become "shots in the arm" to your feelings of importance at all times.

For example, I have observed what happens when certain customers come into the barbershop where I usually go and wait for their favorite barber. Such customers certainly bring bright lights into the days of these barbers. I have watched how the man servicing chair number four feels for a moment more important than the boss at chair number one when someone has picked out his services as being the best in the shop. By the same token, other customers will have their pet preferences for barbers at chair three, two, or one.

There is no question about it: the barber who cuts my hair gives me what I consider to be expert individual attention. He is catering to a satisfaction that thrives on the feeling of importance he gets each time I by-pass his fellow barbers in order to wait my turn with him. His eyes light up each time I come in the door because he knows, no matter how many persons are in the shop I will wait for him.

Here are a few examples of how one man I know accentuates the importance principle to get support toward his own success. Jerry, as a leader of a research group, makes it a point to make off-the-cuff statements that highlight the importance of various members of his staff. I have heard him say in earshot of the persons concerned:

"Mary is the best little paper tester in the shop."

"When I need to get straightened out on something that has to do with organic chemistry Jim is the fellow I go to."

"The things I like most about Helen, my secretary, is that she can just about read my mind. She's just the best doggone secretary a fellow could have."

"Take George here. If he ever got sick on us, I don't know what we would do. He can keep our charges up to date better than one of Uncle Sam's revenue men."

A somewhat similar expression of this delicate yet vital emphasis on the development of a feeling of importance in others came home to me one evening when we were guests at the country residence of a prominent musician. Among the guests there that evening was a physician who was famous throughout the country as a specialist in internal medicine. In the course of the evening, the host announced that he wanted to surprise his guests and entertain them with a skill that he alone knew the distinguished physician possessed. With only this skimpy introduction, the host sat down at the piano and invited his guest to sing several songs while he accompanied him.

The physician had been studying voice for years. At every opportunity, he strove to improve himself at his avocation until he had achieved an outstanding level of perfection. What struck me was the great feeling of importance that suddenly enveloped this distinguished man as he performed at a skill far removed from the profession in which his reputation had been made.

If he had been called upon to try to save the life of a person in the throes of pneumonia, his audience would automatically assume that he would succeed. To them, such an achievement bordered on the routine. It would be the type of accomplishment for which he was famous. But when he had finished several songs, which he sang beautifully, the guests literally brought down the house with their applause. They had discovered something important and unexpected in him. By so doing they opened up an entirely new stairway to his innermost sanctum of importance.

I am sure that this physician for months afterward took much satisfaction from the feeling of importance which his host helped him achieve that evening. Sometime later, my friend told me that he was completely overwhelmed by the messages and the frequent gifts that the physician continued to send him and his wife!

The "Case of the Celebrated Physician" brings out the worthwhile point that there is always a way to make the other fellow feel important, no matter how big, how successful, how important he already is. By so doing, you will win his friendship and make yourself more influential with him.

It is surprising how this principle can be used effectively in all kinds of ways and all kinds of situations. Never miss an opportunity to show the other fellow that you appreciate his abilities, even those for which he does not get formal recognition. If you are the one who gives him recognition that he does not usually expect or receive, he will most likely return the same to you. He will become your most active personal public relations director!

It is true that everyone likes to feel that he is important. But you have to be careful that you don't allow your own drive for this feeling ride roughshod over the same desire on the part of someone who may be more important than you are. At no time, perhaps, is this more clearly illustrated than in your daily contacts with the people with whom you work. Often, it is necessary to be more mindful of the other man's drive, if you expect to succeed in achieving the next, higher rung on the ladder in the satisfaction of your own longing.

Let's consider, for example, the case of the man who receives a promotion into a department that is new to him. This is a rather frequent situation, one you may have run into yourself. Such a

man may suddenly find himself with jurisdiction over people
who actually know more about the specific workings of the department than he does. Unless the people in that department
play their cards right, they find themselves with all kinds of
trouble on their hands.

I recall a man named Henry, a chemist by training, who was
given administrative responsibility over a division concerned
with the research and development of electronic instruments.
The people in this division were physicists. Naturally, they knew
a lot more than Henry did about electronics. But Henry had
proven his ability to lead men and could be expected to become
proficient in the operation of this department in time.

What happened? One of the physicists, a man named Jack,
who reported to the new boss, tried to satisfy his own importance
by showing Henry how much he knew about his field. Every
chance he got, he played up his own knowledge of electronics
and embarrassed Henry for his lack of scientific know-how before his subordinates. Jack thought he was forcing Henry to lean
on him for his administrative decisions. He would make himself
indispensable to the boss by proving that Henry couldn't take a
step unless he came to him for advice. Jack would become the
real leader; he would be the hero, the guiding genius of the division. Before long, he thought, Henry would have to cater to
him in everything he did.

Not surprisingly, Jack found that he got exactly the opposite
of what he expected. Because he tried to satisfy his thirst for importance in the wrong way, he was doomed to failure from the
start. By watering down his boss's abilities in an effort to put the
spotlight on his own, Jack succeeded only in blocking Henry's
chance to quench his own desire for a feeling of importance and
usefulness. All he accomplished was to place a tremendous ob-
stacle in his own path to progress. You can be sure that Henry
did little to push Jack ahead when the opportunity came up.
Jack's own light was doused and he became less important than
he was before. But Henry didn't do it to him; he did it to himself.

Just by way of contrast, consider what happened to one of the
other physicists in Henry's division. This man had an equally
strong drive for a feeling of importance and success. But he

didn't let it blind him to Henry's need for the same kind of satisfaction. Instead of showing up the boss for his lack of electronic experience, he let Henry know, quietly, that he would be glad to help whenever a problem came up. And he did help, in a sincere effort to give Henry a hand. What's more, he kept his mouth shut about it in front of his fellow workers. He did the job management expected him to do, without fanfare. Result? Henry ran the division with exceptional success, the company directors decided to expand the division and to create the post of assistant division manager. Who got the job? You guessed it; the second physicist, who had really become Henry's right-hand man. He made his boss feel important, and, by so doing, satisfied his own drive for success, importance, and position.

This story illustrates clearly how your approach to the other fellow's basic emotions and drives can be a ladder to success or a quick slide into the pit of failure. Accentuating the other man's importance can lead you to victory and an unusual measure of satisfaction and success, just as long as you do not let your own personal desires run away with you. The way to make yourself important is to make the other person important, especially when he really is more important than you are.

One clergyman that I knew, a prominent author and book critic, was a very humble man. Yet at a lecture that I attended, he held up the audience with rather rude indifference. On his way to the lecture hall he was surrounded by a group of young high school boys and girls seeking his autograph. Not until he had signed each autograph request and answered their numerous questions did it ever occur to him, humble man that he was, that he was holding up a bewildered and embarrassed chairman and a luncheon audience of almost one thousand persons. The young high school students clamoring for his autograph were stimulating his subconscious thirst for a public acknowledgement of his importance to such an extent that he became submerged by their attentiveness.

These youngsters, unknowingly perhaps, were applying the "importance principle" to get what they wanted from this normally aloof clergyman with resounding success.

Another man I know, a retired business executive, who earned

$100,000 a year before his retirement, is still a wonderful tennis player. A close friend of mine (several times the winner of a state tennis championship) has made good by using the "importance principle" on this retired executive; he plays tennis with him several times each summer and makes it rather easy for the executive to set up a schedule with my friend on the former's private tennis court.

Recently, my friend told me the following, bringing out once again the great value of putting the "importance principle" into action in your own specific human relationships:

"G. F.," as he refers to the retired executive, "is carried to unusually high plateaus of pleasure each time he succeeds in beating me badly at tennis. To be able to beat a 'champ' at a game from which he also derives much pleasure is adding years to this man's life. Apparently he enjoys telling all of his buddies at the Philadelphia Country Club about his successful tennis bouts with me. This compensates him for the loss of the feeling of importance and power that he used to enjoy before his retirement."

Within two months after I had made a note about this case history for inclusion in this book, I met my friend unexpectedly at an American Management Association meeting. "Just thought you would like to know I've got a new job," he told me. "Old G. F. went out of his way to recommend me for an opening in the company's head office in Philadelphia. I'm now a special staff assistant to the president."

As a lecturer, time and time again, I have found that there is magic in going out of your way to make the other fellow feel more important than you, at least for a moment or two. Pay special attention to the chairman of any gathering before which you may be invited to talk. Do this by trying deliberately to make the chairman feel at ease, and important, even more important than you, the speaker. Believe me, there is no surer way to get a friendly send-off from the chairman of a meeting. When the chairman of any group or conference feels that you are impressed by *his* importance and his good judgment in his selection of you as the speaker, the success of your talk as well as the warmth of your audience are assured.

The success of Edward R. Murrow's famous television program pivots on the application of the importance principle. To realize this, you need only observe how deftly he touches on subjects about the careers of the persons he interviews in order to bring out answers which prove their importance in the eyes of their audience. In your own person-to-person contacts, you too can become a popular "interviewer" if you will choose questions to make the other fellow tell you the things about himself that are the real foundations upon which his appraisal of his own importance rest.

Make People Feel More Important by Your Daily Communications with them

1. Be generous about giving them the full benefit of any titles for which they have qualified. For example, a retired major general I know delights at being addressed as just plain "General" even though he never uses the title himself.
2. Use the friendly, persuasive, and informal telephone approach. Instead of, "Smith speaking," try the magic of, "Bud Smith speaking. What can I do for you?" Or if your caller is someone from whom you have not heard in quite a while, work in, "It's always a pleasure to hear from you."
3. Before asking a fellow employee to do you a favor, or, as his supervisor, telling him to undertake a nasty assignment, use the magic of the "importance principle" to get what you want accomplished. Call it "sugar-coating" the pill if you will, but is it not true that a bad-tasting pill is really no trouble at all to swallow if it is sugar-coated? For a further example, ask a man about the bowling trophy he won the other evening and listen to him tell you about it; then see how he responds to a request you make of him later.

You cannot put yourself on a surer footing to a position of influence with people than by showing *constantly* a genuine interest in their needs, and by thinking and acting in line with what is important to them.

To do this successfully, you must keep reminding yourself about the really important things, those that count most so far as the other fellow is concerned; his family, his job, his home, his health, his security, and even his standing with his neighbors. If you can acquire a genuine interest in the needs of other people, if you can learn to think in terms of what they believe to be important to them, you will completely revitalize your own potential for success.

Vincent R., a physical therapist I know, is an expert in the art of using personal importance to reslant the emotions of some of his most difficult patients. There was the case, for example, of an elderly but wealthy lady who was undergoing physical therapy treatments for a broken hip. This lady was an "impossible" patient; she refused to endure the slightest pain and when she did, she gave Vincent R. a thoroughgoing tongue-lashing. This made Vincent's efforts to get her back on her feet useless.

He then went to work on this difficult patient by applying the importance principle. He had heard that she had, decades ago, met with royalty in England and even dined on several occasions with Queen Mary of England, consort of King George V. She was proud of her English background so Vincent invariably got her to talk about her experiences in England when he began to treat her. She responded admirably and loudly. For she noticed that all the other patients in the room where the walking exercises were given listened to her with awe. And, as she talked on, feeling the thrill of her importance, Vincent succeeded in getting her to walk continuously without a single reference to the pain he knew she was feeling.

So it is in your everyday life. There are many persons who cannot be approached in the usual way. Find out what each of such persons considers to be vitally important to him. Then apply the "importance principle" to win his support and interest over to your side.

Self-Importance Always Spells Boredom and Failure

There is no faster way of driving people away from you than by drenching yourself with your own importance. Not even your best friend can stand never-ending tales of accomplishments that are designed to blow up your own importance. Rather, the subtle habit of encouraging the other fellow to come out of his shell, to speak up about himself, is bound to establish you as a wonderful person, one with boundless tolerance, a person worthy of the very best treatment.

Leonard, owner of a delicatessen, is no longer in business because he "boasted" his customers away. One by one he added signs, like "Leonard the Submarine Sandwich King," to his shop. Then he would deluge each new customer with the boast that people came as far as 25 miles just to buy his sandwiches. One day, when I was in his shop, I heard a customer ask him to add a few extra slices of onion to a sandwich he was making up for him. Leonard turned and growled as though he were in reality a King, of submarine sandwiches. And pity the young lad, with or without a parent, who held the door open a few seconds longer than normal so that a fly or two got in.

Leonard forgot in his preoccupation with patting himself on the back that it was other people, his customers, who paid his bills and kept him in business. His self-importance dried up the lifeline to his bank account because it antagonized his customers; as a result he went out of business.

Frequently, such people, perennial "Ego-spouters," are trying to camouflage something about which they are insecure. If you can encourage such individuals to come out of the shells, you will be gratified at how much good they are capable of doing.

One of the best ways I have found to divert the "boredom" of an ego-spouter is to put him to work. Appoint him to head a committee, ask him to arrange a party in honor of someone, or work to get him elected into some community office. Frequently, energy normally expended ego-wise becomes directed most commendably in behalf of a church project, in improving office morale, or in making a champion Little League Ball Club come into being.

One man I know, Frank, is chairman of numerous professional committees. He enjoys one of the finest reputations in the chemical profession. He is master of the art of making the other person feel important.

But Frank's reputation and wide influence have not developed just because he knows how to delegate responsibility, nor are they merely based on a "passing the buck" policy. Rather, Frank constantly and in all honesty seeks to give the other fellow a chance to be in the limelight whenever something comes up that he cannot handle better on his own. Even when it would be easy for Frank to keep all the glory for himself, he never hesitates to let the other man earn it, because his main purpose is to get the job done best by the best person, and he tries to boost anyone whenever he can. As a result, he is one of the most successful chairmen and executives in the industry, popular with everyone, and phenomenally productive.

Yet people who do things willingly for Frank have repeatedly commented on how unaggressive yet capable he is! Frank commands a prestige that is hard to equal.

Here are a few of his ways of toning himself down and building up the person whose help he seeks:

1. "Look Jim, I couldn't possibly handle this meeting in New York City next February. Since you know so much more about the symposium than I do, won't you please chairman the meeting. I would like *you* to run the show after I give you a brief introduction."

2. "You are by far the best man in the country to edit this report and make a recommendation for a course of action to my committee."

3. "You have been recommended to me as the one man who can get something concrete done about this new standard procedure. How about taking the matter from there for us?"

4. "If there is one thing I can't do well, that is to write good notes about a meeting. Could I impose on you to expend some of your literary talent in behalf of getting a good record of what goes on here today?"

He immediately gets all the support he needs to get the job done. He gives the other fellow a chance to bask at least 90 per cent of the time in the spotlight. But, when all is said and done, the credit comes to him largely because somebody else did a job very well, a job that he would normally have had to do.

It is not, you see, nearly so important for you to get the job done as it is for you to see that the job is done by somebody else, and done right! There is no surer way of getting lots of jobs done than by making many other people feel it is important to them to want to do the job for you! This is why the use of the understatement in your behalf, the use of the truth to bring out the necessary feeling of importance in the other fellow, can become a magic technique for reaching your objectives, and increasing your power over people to boot!

Today, make a special effort to observe how many people with whom you come into contact are touchy, easily insulted, and bitter. Notice how numerous people seem to go through life with set jaws, strained facial expressions and tense muscles. These people have had their exposed egos severely bruised. They are so vulnerable that they wince at the slightest insult, are wound up as tense as a watchspring. Why? They have not succeeded in satisfying their thirst for a feeling of importance, even partially within their own limited sphere of influence.

Since such people do exist in large numbers, you must learn how to cope with them, or they will make inroads into your own success and happiness. To cope with such negative personalities, you must begin by giving them honest recognition for their real accomplishments so that they will regain their feeling of being somebody important. They, in turn, will make you important and successful by doing things for you, recommending you to others, and boosting you to friends.

The case of Peter, a lone-wolf insurance and real estate agent, is a good one to show you what can happen when steps are taken to wipe out the stress in an individual who goes through life like a taut watchspring.

Peter's main source of stress was a slight crippling in his left leg from arthritis, which forced him to walk with a slight limp. He was sensitive about this, acting as though he were the only person in the world singled out to be so plagued. His emotional stress reflected itself in his curt mannerisms and his sometimes belligerent behavior.

When I first met Peter, I wondered how he ever managed to obtain or hold onto any business. Then one day I happened to stop in at his office with a friend whose badly damaged car had been insured through Peter.

As we sat down, my friend turned toward me and, as an aside, said, "Now, if you want to see a man in action who really places the interests of his customers first and foremost, just watch Peter go to work on my case."

I could see the stress fade out of Peter's muscles as soon as my friend had spoken. Peter's face lit up with a smile as he reached over and dialed the local claim agent of the insurance company concerned. He handled the negotiations with professional skill and got the necessary paperwork rolling by taking obvious shortcuts.

Later, my friend told me how pleased he was with the speed and amount of the settlement. I eventually transferred my own automobile insurance policies over to Peter's care. And by mentioning my admiration of the way Peter handles claims, I have managed to bring him out of his shell in his dealings with me at least. Peter, like most of us, gladly sets aside the things that prick his ego and build up stress within as soon as he sees an occasion or a person permitting him to bring out a skill or ability that demonstrates something unique or praiseworthy about himself.

You, too, can change porcupines into possums by helping others to give wings to the stresses that normally keep them in mental straight-jackets. To do this, you must evaluate each such problem-contact, and cultivate a full feeling of tolerance and understanding for the numerous drives prodding the other fellow just as they are prodding you. By so doing you will be cultivating a trait within yourself that will help you to reach new heights of popularity and success in your dealings, especially with obstinate people.

What the "Importance Drive" Can Do in Your Daily Human Contacts

If you have ever had the experience of getting slow and uninspired service from a waiter, try this: next time you're in a diner on the train, see what happens when you say to the steward when he hands you the menu, "How do you people manage to handle so many customers so fast in such a small area? It always amazes me to see how you serve such delicious meals under the difficult conditions you have to meet. You must have a terrific system."

Do not be surprised if you get the fastest, most efficient service you have ever received. That steward will go out of his way to show you that his system really is terrific. After all, he is not going to prove to you that you are wrong about him. You have made him feel that he is doing something outstanding and important. You both gain; he feels great, and you get a fine meal in jig time.

The next time you need a shoeshine on a battered pair of shoes, watch what happens when you tell the shoeshine boy, "Now here is a pair of shoes to which I am especially attached. They're very comfortable to wear. I'll bet you know what to do to get me extra mileage out of them and make them look like new, too."

Of course, you will not get the routine, superficial treatment. He will clean the shoes, get the loose dirt out of the inaccessible cracks, and put extra elbow grease into the shining. And he'll be proud when you step down from his stand and you can see your face reflecting from the sheen on your "battered" pair of shoes.

Some time ago, I told a Philadelphia custom hat maker that he did a professional job of selecting a hat to fit my head and to suit my facial features and build. Now, when I go into his store I can count on him literally dropping everything to give me the full benefit of his experience, advice, and assistance.

The next time you are in a hotel see what happens when you tell the bellhop he looks like a Canadian Mountie in his snappy uniform as he leads you to your room. You will be astounded at the service and information he will volunteer.

Tell the druggist you are relying on his expert judgment to recommend the newest toothpaste or the best antiacid preparation and you probably will find yourself overwhelmed by his intense desire to prove to you that he knows the best answers for all your drugstore needs. Moreover, he will go out of his way to call special bargains to your attention.

Tell the young lady or young man who is checking-out at the supermarket that the last time you were there he packed your order so well not a single bag tore on you; there is no surer way to get the checker to go to the greatest possible pain to do his job as he is supposed to do it.

In your own home, of course, giving the children or your wife the attention that they need and deserve so that they can feel they are important cogs in the family wheel is of the utmost importance. You can achieve excellent results in numerous ways. See what happens to your own little girl when you tell her you know of no better way to soothe your tired body than to relax in a living room chair and listen to her play the piano. I have done this, and what a thrill it is to have a tiny pair of hands grab mine after dinner, lead me into a comfortable chair, prop my feet up on a footrest, and then perform most diligently for me.

And, ever since I told an important guest how helpful my young son (who was beside me at the time) had been by keeping my shoes shined and my office wastebasket emptied, I have been delighted repeatedly to find him come into my office at home on a Saturday morning and, without any bidding on my part, empty the week's load from the wastebaskets. And now and then a couple of pairs of shoes show up beside my bed shined professionally!

When your wife painstakingly sews one of her own dresses, or makes a suit, see what happens when you tell her, "I don't think I've ever seen a prettier suit or dress in Saks Fifth Avenue; you've done a beautiful job." Not only will you be paying her a compliment she has rightfully earned, but you will find that your wife will make more suits and dresses just to please you. Of course, the family budget will be helped, as a minor repercussion, but the important thing is that both you and your wife will gain satisfaction from a willingly directed creative effort.

Always remember that a person's importance is an edifice that must be rebuilt everyday. You have within you the power to make the housemaid feel on top of the world, at least for a time, just as you can make a corporation president feel more important even though his position of importance already is very high.

The "importance" about which I have written in this chapter is, to be sure, a relative thing. As a parallel example, a man with little money can feel very wealthy when he suddenly inherits a thousand dollars, but, on the other hand, if another man who already has a million dollars inherits a large sum by average standards, it is unlikely that he will experience the same intensity of happiness and delight.

You cannot make a comedian happy by paying him a large salary alone; you can only make him happy by laughing at his jokes, too! A comedian feels he is important, not in proportion to the salary he collects, but rather in proportion to the applause he can command! That is true of each of us in every walk of life. What really counts in the end is the applause that we think we can see, feel, or hear, the applause that comes into our hearts from the people around us. This kind of applause is one of the most important rewards we receive throughout life.

When I consider the tremendous consequences that can be derived from the littlest things, like a chance word, a pat on the shoulder, a smile, a bow, a tip of the hat, or a well-earned compliment, I realize that these are real seeds of popularity and success so completely ignored by most of us.

These words from the play *Brigadoon* should often come back to all of us, " 'Tis the hardest thing in the world to give everything even though 'tis the only way to get everything."

We might paraphrase these significant words by saying, "It is the hardest thing in the world to make the other fellow feel more important than you are, even though it is the best way to get the world on your side and to put as many people as you may choose to work for you."

Satisfy the other fellow's deep-rooted drive to want to feel important about at least one little ability or possession and you will become an important person yourself, one who can strongly influence the actions and reactions of others.

Learn the key things to sprinkle in your everyday conversation; this will make others remember *you* for years because of what you said about *their* importance.

Self-importance, the handicap that comes with ego-spouting,

always spells failure when it comes to moving people to act in your behalf. It is the fellow who on numerous occasions deliberately takes a back seat that keeps actual control of the steering wheel.

7.

For a More Powerful Personality, Control the Emotions and Attitudes of Others

---

WE ARE ALL SUBJECT TO THE POWER OF EMO-
tions, especially the other fellow's! But you can control the attitudes and emotions of the people with whom you must work and
live so that they will help you, not hurt or hinder you. And, also,
you can control and discipline your own emotions so they will
put new power into your hands.

Conflicting emotions and an explosive attitude can and do
frequently upset the boat of successful human relations, as
Ralph B. came to learn the hard, sad way.

Ralph was a hard-hitting supervisor. He had a reputation for
expecting much from all who reported to him. And despite his
uncompromising stands at times, he was popular with the
people in the department he had supervised for over five years.
They knew that Ralph, beneath his energetic and somewhat
demanding outer shell, really was devoted to his staff. They knew
he would go to bat to get them raises when they deserved them,
and back them up when they needed his backing.

But Ralph's troubles did not begin until he was transferred to supervise a different department when his company began a policy of rotating supervisors. He made his mistake the first day he took over the reins of the department to which he had been transferred.

A pair of pipe fitters were fixing a leak in a line in an area of Ralph's new department when he first arrived. Within easy earshot of where the repairs were being done were several girl technicians. When Ralph examined the flimsy repair job that the goldbricking pipe fitters had done he "blew his top," something he seldom permitted himself to do. He bawled them out, and ordered them to rip out what they had done and repair the leak in a more satisfactory manner. But, granted he was a bit on edge because of the normal anxiety that comes with the first day or two of taking over the supervision of a new group of people, Ralph's steam-letting behavior had an immediate and almost disastrous reaction upon the girl technicians who heard it. Two of them promptly reported to personnel and asked for their termination pay. Why? "We don't intend to work for a boss who blows his top like that!" The result was a man-to-man talk between Ralph and his immediate supervisor. Ralph's prior good record as a supervisor held him in good stead. But he was told in no uncertain terms that he had better control his attitude and emotions under irritating circumstances in the future.

Ralph, of course, knew better, but just this once he failed *to control* his own emotions, and invited all kinds of trouble. He even got himself off to a very bad start on a new job, a black mark of no mean proportions that he would live down only after months of excellent performance.

Imagine how much easier Ralph's new job would have been to him right from the start, how his popularity could have been protected and insured, if only he had "counted ten" when he saw the patched-up job the pipe fitters had done? Nothing will pull the rug from underneath your hard-earned chances for greater success like a failure on your part to discipline your emotional impulses, especially under circumstances when such control can make you stand out and move up ahead.

USE POSITIVISM TO CHASE THE OTHER FELLOW'S
NEGATIVE EMOTIONS

We all know people who like to take the argumentative side of every issue. They enjoy arguing with bus drivers or department store clerks. They are constantly brandishing that chip on their shoulder: "He can't tell me what to do!" "What do you have to be, the governor of the state to get service in this store?"

People who act like this suffer from emotional insecurity or immaturity. They can be completely transformed into likable persons only if you learn to steer their emotions along more positive lines by remote control. They usually will fight every attempt, however, on your part if you set out to influence them in any outward or aggressive manner.

Donald was a young man who worked in a large Philadelphia department store. He was very efficient at his work, but he was also emotionally immature, keeping to himself too much. His advancement was seriously hindered as a result. He would sit by as others were promoted. And each time this would happen, Donald felt that he had been cheated and that people were scheming against him. His disposition grew more solemn, more withdrawn, and more dangerous to him as the months rolled by.

Still later, he began to suffer from internal upsets. For a while, it was feared he was developing a heart condition; his heart palpitated oddly at times. Yet Donald's trouble was entirely emotional. Nobody took enough interest in him to set his emotional balance straight.

It was not until a new acquaintance, in the same department, came along with a happy-go-lucky disposition and a very positive and optimistic outlook on life that Donald was brought out of his shell. By associating with this man, Donald gradually began to give wings to his negative emotions. He began to duplicate his new-found friend's disposition and lively personality. It was no time before his department manager noticed the difference. As a result, he took a greater personal interest in him. Donald's turn for a major promotion came along quickly.

Quite by circumstance, and fortunately for Donald, the negativism with which his personality had become encircled was not neutralized until someone bubbling with positivism came into his life and put his emotions and attitudes on course.

But you can apply this principle of *positivism* deliberately to meet difficult situations in your everyday life. You are a sales clerk and you encounter a gruff, skeptical customer (and there are so many of them!). He frowns at you and in a demanding tone of voice asks for a Dacron-rayon shirt of tinted light-blue, size 15¼ collar, sleeve-length 32⅝ inches, etc. etc. You know it is unlikely that you have anything that will match his demands exactly.

I listened to a sales clerk in the men's department at John Wanamaker's handle such a customer successfully through a truly professional application of the principle of positivism.

"There is a good chance," said the sales clerk, "that we have what you have asked for. I'll be happy to show all that we have coming anywhere close to what you are seeking." With gusto the sales clerk began stacking shirts before his gruff customer, and with equal gusto I listened to him discharge *positivism:* "I enjoy serving someone like you, sir, who knows exactly what he is in search of. Aren't the new synthetic blends wonderful, though? My wife keeps blessing the chemist who invented these new easy-to-wash shirts. We do have just at this time the best inventory of shirts that we have had in months."

Soon Mr. Gruff Customer was comparing three shirts side-by-side—white, light-grey, and light-pink! The light-pink one had caught his fancy, so much so that he forgot he had originally insisted on seeing a light blue one. "You know," I heard him say smilingly to the sales clerk, "my wife gave me a tie for my birthday this past week that will go especially well with this one!" He was pointing to the tinted pink shirt, and that was the one with which he walked out of the store.

Positivism can, indeed, put *your* emotions on course, change them inside out. There is no other successful way to emerge from a difficult negative situation than through the appropriate application of positivism in such instances.

EMOTIONS ARE AS CONTAGIOUS AS MEASLES:
USE ONE EMOTION TO SPARK ANOTHER

One emotion inevitably sparks another. It is amazing how frequently the emotion of rebuff on the part of one person will be a duplicate of the same emotion in another who is nearby. It also is equally true that humor, for example, at a crucial point in a tense situation can suddenly change the whole atmosphere from one of frustration and hate into one of laughter and friendliness.

I recall walking along a tree-lined street once with my mother-in-law, when, much to my embarrassment and annoyance, a dropping from a bird en route landed on the coat of a brand new suit. My first reaction was one of annoyance, but my mother-in-law came to my rescue and gave my mounting negative emotion a quick flip-flop with, "Just be glad that cows don't fly!"

The underlying principle of this example is, of course, that you can avoid untold unpleasantness, avert quarrels, and maintain a peaceful, pleasant way of life by cultivating and using humor.

Here are a few additional instances when humor has worked like magic to spark a situation-saving response:

1. Your youngster spills a glass of ginger ale on your table-cloth and stands aghast, expecting a tongue-lashing. You curb your natural emotion response and quickly observe: "Well, Bill, I am thankful, at least, that you don't drink ink!"

2. An employee comes to you emotionally upset and on the verge of tears. You aren't quite sure what her trouble is, but you know that you are not involved. You quip before she gets a chance to spill her woes all over you: "Don't tell me you let the stapler fall on your big toe again!"

3. The garage attendant inadvertantly lets gas overflow on to your rear fender. Your temperature spurts up, but you curb your anger and say instead, "I could travel across

country on the amount of overflow gasoline you chaps have made me pay for!"

In each of these instances, and in similar ones, humor instead of heat-words can leave you in an unruffled frame of mind, and at the same time correct an obviously irritating situation by adding to your power of influence with the persons concerned.

When it comes to controlling the other fellow's emotions, one of your biggest assets is the way you wear your face, literally. Few people appreciate the fact that the human face can speak louder than words. Your eyes, your smile, your conscience are constantly revealing messages to the other person. These messages are picked up by his built-in tuning system. As Shakespeare has said, "There is no art to find the mind's construction in the face," or as Isaiah the prophet put it, "The show of their countenances have testified against them."

Yes, it is from your face, not your lips, that your soul speaks to other people. Study your face in a mirror often. The practice will surprise you and do you a world of good. Each time you do this, remind yourself that the other fellow sees you just as a mirror does; only he also sees far below your skin, into your heart and conscience. So, cultivate your facial expressions; they are among the least-developed assets you own.

It has been my experience that other people take a far greater interest in your facial expression than in what you are wearing or what you are saying. Your facial expression is a greater force than your hidden bank account, or the price tag on your clothes, your car, your home! Time and time again, some of the most elegantly and fashionably dressed people I have known failed to leave favorable impressions; they fell absolutely flat on their sullen faces. They did not realize that a positive, appealing facial expression can be used to make capital gains with other people.

Consider the case of John, an office manager in an insurance firm. John is so well-dressed that people say he always gives you the impression he is about to go to a wedding or a funeral! But John's dress is restricted only to his clothes. He always wears a facial expression that makes you think he is choking on sour grapes or that his stomach has just had a hole punched in it. He is anything but popular with his staff, despite his impeccable dress. People will never like a person for the price of his clothes nearly as much as for the warmth which radiates from his eyes and the expression on his face.

Frank, on the other hand, is an executive who is really well-dressed. Not only are his clothes always in the best taste; he is a reliably jovial fellow and his full-moon face seems always to be shining just for you. You cannot ever approach Frank or be near him without sensing a positive surge in your emotions. Of course, he is effective in running his department. His department has the least turnover, the least personnel gripes, and the most productivity in his company. Everybody keeps saying behind Frank's back, "He's going to be president of the company some day," even though the chances are Frank has not given that objective too much thought himself.

What does Frank do that John does not to capitalize literally on his face?

Frank even smiles when he is talking long distance on the telephone! He told me once that he was certain that a person listening to his voice hundreds of miles away could sense instinctively that he was smiling as he talked because he really was.

It is as delightful to look into Frank's eyes as it is to listen to his voice. I have never yet caught him frowning at anybody, or looking depressed. Even the day he got a telephone call that his 85-year-old father had passed away in his sleep, I remember how Frank with tear-filled eyes said to me with a warm smile on his face, "It is wonderful, in a way, because Dad always said a man of his age could never hope to be luckier than to bow out as gently as if he were falling asleep."

Frank would never even let the weather dampen the cheerfulness of his facial expression. Caught in a heavy downpour, he said, standing with his hair disheveled and his wet clothes pulled close to his body, "This is supposed to be a wash-and-wear suit. Well, I've been wearing it for sometime, and now it has been washed!"

Frank, unlike John, was a man who lived for others, whose mind was bent on love, not hate, whose thinking was extrovert rather than introvert. You, too, can develop a magnetic facial charm, similar to Frank's, capable of radiating and initiating pleasant emotions in others. For few things can help you to greater success in dealing with people than a lively facial expression. It can make you as welcome and popular as the warmth and glow of logs burning in an open fireplace are on a cold winter day.

One day I saw a lady use her facial expression to achieve an opposite effect from Frank's friendly all-over approach. A burly driver had inadvertently backed into her car and dented a fender. He got out of his car fuming at her, even though the blame for the minor collision was obviously entirely his.

The lady, poised and pretty, stared the loud-mouthed bully into silence. Gradually his voice toned down, and as the lady walked toward him, without saying a word, and keeping the same uncompromising stare, Mr. Loud Mouth was speaking like a gentleman and reaching into his pocket for his driver's license. The facial expression on this woman's face was charged with so much dignity and a sense of righteousness that the man changed face himself, owned up to his mistake, and promised to pay promptly for the damage, slight as it was, he had done to the strange lady's car. The two parted on friendly terms, but the point of this lady's exercise of a disciplinary facial expression is that she did not relax it and replace it with a more friendly view until she was sure she had more than won her case, and that little was to be gained by prolonging the other person's professed guilt.

You Can Predict Human Nature and Plot Your Course with People

Have you ever noticed how often you have said something only to regret a moment or two later having said it because by so doing you unleashed unpleasantness on the part of another? The fact is that you can frequently anticipate how a person will react to what you may say or do. To be influential in your dealings with people you must weigh your words and actions carefully so that they will bring you positive, friendly responses instead of uncooperative, even nasty ones. Yet it is the neglect of this simple and oft-proven principle that gives rise to some of the most serious problems in human relations.

A moment's reflection on your experiences in recent weeks will tell you that you can predict with an accuracy bordering on certainty exactly how your boss will react to a compliment, how your wife will react to a ten-dollar bill you give her to spend "anyway she pleases," how your children will react to a bedtime story you make up on the spur of the moment, how your mother-in-law will react to an unexpected kiss on the forehead when you meet her, even how your dog will react to a few moments of attention and flattering words! But so many of us, even though we realize the truthfulness of being able to control the other person's emotions, transgress this principle with utter disregard.

Make a study of the following case histories which illustrate the principle and technique of how to bring out the best emotional responses in others. You can use solutions to similar situations to protect your own reputation and add to the influence you enjoy over others.

Case I: Speak No Evil; Spread Only the Good

Jim is the most popular fellow in the accounting department of a Philadelphia insurance firm. During the morning coffee break, or during the lunch hour, Jim is at work dispelling derogatory statements about people, things, or places. His philosophy is that the world is big enough for only the *best* of everything. "Talk up the good about a fellow, the other fellow and you spread good into the hearts even of those who are bent on being bad." When a company policy is knocked, Jim is in backing it up. When a department manager is criticized for this or that, Jim is praising him for that or this. Jim's philosophy even carries over to his relationship with his neighbors. One day, when a widow met him on the street and tried to tell him that another neighbor, a widower, had taken to drink, Jim immediately sidetracked her by asking, "Don't you really look fine though since you went over to that new diet you were telling my wife about!" By forcing the conversation away from the widower to a matter of deep personal interest to the widow, Jim cut short what would have been a useless, derogatory conversation that would have added not one word or thought of good to his world. People who know Jim have long ago given up trying to drag him into any kind of derogatory participation, and he enjoys a power over people all his own for being a stalwart crusader of the good word only.

Case 2: Never Criticize the Religious Beliefs of Another

Henry was a deeply religious man, but he believed firmly in a "hands off" policy if people chose to profess religious beliefs that differed from, or even opposed, his own. As a supervisor, he became faced with the problem of a young man on his staff, Jerry, who was outspokenly anti-Catholic as well as anti-Negro. When Jerry's performance review came up, Henry decided to show Jerry how unpopular his outspoken anti-religious and anti-racial comments were making him.

"Jerry," Henry told him, "you feel quite strongly, I am sure, about the way other men should treat your lovely sister, Jane. As a matter of fact, I know that you would let out all the stops if any young man ever said anything distasteful or derogatory about her. Well, have you ever realized that some people have equally strong devotion to the religion of their own choice? Do you know that your outspoken criticism of the religion to which some of your associates adhere is building up within them a deep resentment toward you? Your chances of getting ahead around here will evaporate with what little popularity you have left unless you change your policy. Let each man enjoy his own convictions in matters of religion or you will trespass onto a mine field of trouble. Nothing can ruin a man's friendship and trust faster than religious or racial intolerance. If you can't say a good word for another's religious belief or nationality, the very least you can do to protect your own security is say nothing."

Case 3: Nothing Will Weaken Your Influence Over Others
Like Being a Bore Yourself

Grace is a miserable girl, an unpopular store clerk if ever I
have encountered one. She is typical of the kind of person who
can develop an endless series of new ailments. It is no wonder
she is separated from her husband, and her friends give her
about as much berth as they would a contagious germ. Grace
fails to realize that others abhor the way she tries to call attention to herself, the way she basks in the shadow of her imag-
inary illnesses while boring anybody whose ears she can catch
with endless details about them. Once you try to make yourself
the target of those you think you are trying to please, you will
slip into the isolation ward of popularity. Avoid making a bore
of yourself at all costs; nothing arouses a more distasteful reaction in the emotions of your friends, with the result of a more
decisive blow to your influence with them.

Case 4: Beware of the Holier-Than-Thou Stigma of
Perfectionmania

I have yet to discover a perfectionist type of person who is
very successful in dealing with people. It is human nature to shy
away from a perfectionist: we may admire perfectionism in an
artist or singer, but most of us ordinary human beings are fully
aware that we are all paddling the same imperfect canoe through
life. We resent perfectionism in others who are likely to be as imperfect as we are ourselves. The accountant, the chemist, the
cashier, or the store manager who bristles with outward signs of
perfectionism not only are unpopular as a rule, but they have
usually dug themselves into a rut out of which few friends will
help them. They have little positive influence with anyone.

Case 5: Never *Demand* That Your Importance Be Acknowledged

I know a retired lieutenant general who has gone to such extremes to make people address him as "General," and almost
stand at attention to boot, that he lives a miserably lonely life.
You cannot *make* people recognize your importance: they will

do so only with their own consent. The department head who pounds his desk and emphasizes, "I want you to know I run things around here," is, in all probability a misfit, a man who should never have been promoted to the job he has in the first place. We can paraphrase Biblical advice: "See you first the other fellow's importance, and all your own needs will take care of themselves."

When you act as though you are as important as you may believe you are, all you do is draw an emotion of disgust from others. You can be truly important only when you behave in such a manner that causes others to want to carry you onto the stage entirely on their own power!

If you want to control human emotions and plot your best course with people, remember the following five keys to the successful use of this principle:

1. Spread only the good word.
2. Never show contempt for the religious beliefs of others.
3. Never weaken your influence with people by being a bore yourself.
4. Beware of the holier-than-thou Stigma of Perfectionmania.
5. Never *demand* that your importance be acknowledged by others.

USE PERSUASION TO SWAY THE EMOTIONS AND ATTITUDES OF OTHERS

A man I know is a clerk in a sales office. He has been at this job for over ten years. On the surface, it had appeared to his supervisor that he lacked the personality and drive to be promoted to the sales force. Yet, one of this clerk's secret ambitions for years had been to become a successful salesman.

Then, one day, he confided to his supervisor his ambition to qualify for the sales force some day. With this lead to go on, the clerk's boss took a greater interest in helping him to overcome the negative emotional attitude which was holding him in check. Gently, he guided this clerk into acquiring the polish and the controlled extrovert characteristics which he knew he needed if he were to become a successful salesman.

The clerk's boss persuaded him to enroll in a local public speaking course. He arranged for him next to become active in PTA meetings where the lessons he learned about public speaking could be tested in the open. The transformation in the clerk was steady. His supervisor had brought him a long way toward his goal through the painstaking and persistent use of the gentle art of persuasion. After the clerk had shown ample evidence that he had developed enough poise, self-confidence, and flexibility in dealing with people, the supervisor set up an interview for him with the company's sales manager. It was a success. Soon this clerk was graduated into the sales force where the persuasive supervisor had the satisfaction of seeing a man he had helped achieve a secret ambition, and his company acquire from within a capable salesman who would add much to the annual sales tally.

I cannot think of a more important time to influence human emotions favorably than when you want to put across your idea. How you go about controlling the attitudes and emotions of the people upon whom you must rely to get your ideas across can often mean the difference between outstanding success and utter failure.

Most of us make the sad mistake of failing to use a suitable story plot in timing our control of the emotions of others. A good idea, if properly developed, can sell itself to your listeners with the same effectiveness as a good mystery story, which entrances its readers when the timing of each clue and each step of the narrative is adroitly handled by an experienced author.

There is quite a parallel between good writing, and the manner by which it influences the emotions of a reader, and good human relations, and the manner in which they influence the emotions of those who listen to you. After all, the quickest way for a mystery writer to end up in the poorhouse is to begin his stories by giving his clues and the outline of the story plot in the first paragraph!

The most effective way to capture and control the emotions of those to whom you wish to sell your ideas is to build each point of your case slowly. First, you present your idea in a toned-down manner. Then you analyse it with your listeners. You list its weaknesses and also alternate ideas that are not quite as good but which ought to be weighed, too. But you purposely keep the meat of your idea, its punch-line, as a climax for your audience. It is during your wind-up, your summation, that you play your trump card. This keeps the emotions and interest of your listeners tuned to your way of thinking to the very end. The fellow who "blows his bolt" in one surge may wind up adding fuel to the other fellow's flaming desire to discredit his ideas and their value.

John C. is especially capable in using proper timing in presenting new ideas to his people. He can keep them in suspense and keep their interest high so that when he needs to get their consent he has full control over their emotions and attitudes.

I recall one occasion when, as the vice president for manufacturing for his company, he was faced with the difficult task of announcing a ten per cent cut in the salaries of all on the monthly payroll, because of a slump in business that did not show any immediate signs of easing up.

The skill with which this man led up to the crux of his task a step at a time was of professional calibre. He called his technical staff together. The first thing he did was painstakingly describe for them the exact profit and loss picture for their company in recent months. It wasn't good. Next he embarked on an optimistic picture for the future; research had several exciting new products about a year or two away; customer inventories of their existing products should reach rock-bottom in about six months, and an upswing could be expected some time after that. The fact remained, however, that at the moment the company was losing about $1,000,000 a month and the Board of Directors requested management to take appropriate steps to save the stockholders' money! Rather than lay people off, management decided to have faith in an upswing within a year or two. However, until such time as the profit picture returned to a normal level for the company—and now he came to the object of his conditioning remarks—it was decided that all members of supervision from the president down would be forced to take a ten per cent cut in salary.

This manufacturing vice president succeeded in getting his staff to accept this "bitter pill" by taking care in leading up to it, by conditioning his audience for a favorable emotional response to it, and by timing the actual announcement of it for the most appropriate psychological moment. Imagine what bedlam would have resulted, what loss of efficiency and *esprit de corps* would have befallen his staff, if he had simply issued a blanket memorandum announcing the ten per cent cut in salary!

In addition to using the "plot," or careful timing sequence, to get your points across in the most favorable manner, you will find that you can sometimes change the other man's attitude toward you by asking him for help. When you go to a person with the idea that you *know* he or she can solve your problem, you'll be astonished at the results. Then, too, it is amazing how often, just by admitting that you *need* help, you can turn the emotions of a bitter opponent inside-out and bring him to your support.

I recall a barber in my own home town who had enjoyed a very excellent business for many years. One day a young man from a different community opened a barber shop within a stone's throw of the older barber. The newcomer began to win over many of the customers who up to that time patronized the older barber. Soon the older barber felt the pinch financially. His rage mounted as his pride and his pocketbook began to suffer. In a futile effort to strike back at his young competitor he began accusing him of price cutting and slander.

The young barber, however, had a most unusual reply for his customers when they came to him and mentioned the tongue-wagging that the older barber was making against him. The younger barber simply refused to fight back. His stock reply was, "I can't understand it. I know Joe is a much better barber than I am. As a matter of fact, I believe he is the finest barber in town! Someday I hope to become as good as he is."

It was not long before the compliments of the younger barber quieted the hostile comments of the older barber. And then, the younger barber, sensing that Joe was gradually losing his animosity towards him, did the most unexpected thing. He called on Joe, one day, and actually asked him for help. He needed money, he explained, to buy another barber's chair so he could hire some help. Would Joe be kind enough to loan him the money at six per cent?

Not only was Joe flattered, and not only did he loan his young competitor the money, but he went much farther than that. What had been an emotion of hate soon mellowed; in the face of a plea for help it changed into an emotion of love and paternal concern. In time, the two men became fast friends. Before the old barber retired he took this newcomer into his shop. When he died he left his entire business to him.

Imagine what a constant and intense battle would have raged if the younger barber had not used kindness to control the emotions of his competitor? What a different ending this story would have had if the younger man had resorted to slander and caustic comments to fight back at the old fellow whose ego had been hurt, or if he had been too proud to seek help from the one person who had tried to hurt his reputation.

All through your life you will find that sweetness always overpowers sourness. The best way to fight the other fellow's emotions, to win them to your side, is never to criticize your enemies. Only say things and do things that will make the person who is trying to hurt you be right! When you go to the support of the position that an enemy takes you are literally digging up by the roots the very source of his antagonism and planting the seed of love and friendship in the hole left behind. When you ask an enemy for help you are apt to achieve two purposes in one blow; destroy an enemy, and acquire a real friend who will defend you with calculated conscientiousness.

Another very important point to remember in connection with emotions and human relations is that a gripe has a very high emotional price tag attached to it. If you engage in griping or gossiping, you are expending emotional energy and jeopardizing your happiness. At best, the reward for spreading gossip or complaining is shallow. If you only devote such emotional energy toward making yourself or others happy, you will put a sparkle into your life and your personality completely overshadowing whatever weakness you possess.

Some of the most exhausted (and exhausting) persons I have ever known are those who have given vent to that human emotion which encourages griping or gossiping hours on end. All too often, such back-knifing is against the selfsame people who have done so much to put the gripers where they are. At the end of a gripe session, the people who are the participants always emerge with drawn faces and an exhausted look. In return for selling some other person's character downstream, all their bitter verbal butchering succeeds in doing is to shave away the veneer of their own self-respect.

Do everything you can to obtain a reputation as one who refuses to traffic in gripes and gossip. You will, with such a reputation, acquire full control over the more favorable emotional responses of the people with whom you have to work. There is no surer way to gain the trust, respect, and loyalty of people in your business or personal life. If people know you are not the "gossip" type, they are bound to share their confidences with you more openly as well as go out of their way to enjoy your company and association.

Anger, of course, is one of the most violent emotions. I dare say there are few of us who haven't been sorry for saying harsh words, those which raised the temperature of those at whom they were directed. By the same token, I don't know of anyone who has not been glad and happy for having been outspoken in the use of soft, reasonable words and tones. In all of my experience I cannot recall a single successful person who was not famous for his calm temperament, his patience, and ever-steady control of his temper.

Unfortunately, we all pass off too lightly the way we ordinarily strive to make a point or try to protect our rights from being trampled. Actually, getting the other fellow's fighting blood up is usually the longest and hardest way to get somewhere. As Woodrow Wilson said, "If you come to me with your fists doubled I think I can promise you that mine will double as fast as yours." This, of course, is a version of the old truism, "Action and reaction are equal and opposite."

But it does not have to be this way. You can be a quick-tempered Irishman like Jim Q. and still learn always to speak softly and carry a big stick!

The only time I have ever heard Jim Q. give full vent to his temper was when I played golf with him and he sliced a new ball into a wooded area. Then, fortunately, ladies would be absent and the wind was usually agin him. The people who worked under Jim had no idea as to the heights to which his temper could rise or the breadth of his unprintable vocabulary!

On the job, Jim Q. is a "proper Bostonian," a polite gentleman in the finest tradition. I dare say someone could spill a bottle of ink on his new suit and he would emerge good-humored and unruffled from it all.

"I made up my mind a long time ago" Jim told me, "that the most expensive treat a man can give himself is to tell another person exactly what he thinks of him! Ever since, I confine venting my anger on things, *never* on people. My golf club, or the powermower I can't get started, have a way of taking all I can give them squarely on the chin. And when I've said my piece, I feel just as good about it as if I had dressed down the Chief of Police, without any of the dreadful consequences that almost always result from getting angry with anybody, shoeshine boy to high school principal."

Jim Q. has a gold mine for you in his philosophy. All of us do need to release the "safety valve" now and then to recover our balance from distressing things that people do. But let the old steam scald a radiator cover, a jalopy, or what have you, and never a person. Certainly it may take some extra effort on your part to do something nice for the other fellow, especially when you may be inclined to believe he does not deserve it. Yet, there is no straighter road to your own success than the one whereby you go out of your way to persuade rather than upset people, getting others to agree friend-like rather than disagree enemy-like. Only by deliberately creating an atmosphere of emotional calmness and stability will you ever succeed at keeping other people agreeable and interested in doing anything they can to promote your personality and boost you to success.

Of course, the emotion of anger sometimes can have a certain amount of value. Anger, whether evidenced in another person or given vent by yourself, can sometimes open up doors of opportunity. It can also help to break the grip that harmful habits may have on you. There is, perhaps, some truth in the belief that unless the average individual gets angry once in a while he will have difficulty in keeping his sanity in this slipshod world of ours.

But working up a head of steam can mean real progress only if it is well directed. The man who invented the stethoscope was a physician who got hopping mad at having to listen to the heartbeat of patients by putting his ear against dirty chests infested with lice. The inventor of the pneumatic tire became incensed each time he saw his son ride over rough gravel roads on his steel-wheeled bicycle. He feared for the safety of his boy's spinal column.

Hundreds of cases in history, as well as in everyday life, could be rounded up to demonstrate that it takes a well-intentioned head of steam to get something done right or make a giant step forward. Certainly, it is most unlikely that the atom bomb would have been perfected in America at the time it was if Hitler and Pearl Harbor had not forced America to build up the kind of steam pressure that caused the creation of the Manhattan project.

Nevertheless, the truth remains that the happiest and most successful people are those who are able to let their emotion of love win over their emotion of anger. In the battle of emotions, the unhappy, the grouchy, and the discouraged are nearly always the least successful. Nothing strangles your chances for success in influencing people like a reputation for being explosive! Such persons are treated like live volcanos because people get to know that they may erupt at anytime; they are given a wide berth and a minimum of cooperation.

HOW TO COPE WITH THOSE INEVITABLE PERSONALITY CLASHES

Inevitably, into each person's life must come people who spontaneously "go against the grain," people you must force yourself to like. The reasons for this still are not understood, but nobody will deny that the situation exists. Frequently it is necessary for you to live or work with someone who, often for mysterious reasons, is a constant source of irritation to you.

For example, a top executive once confided to me, "Jim is and always has been a thorn in my side." This statement startled me. Jim was one man upon whom the executive in question relied most heavily.

"What you just said about Jim doesn't make sense to me," I said. The executive replied, "Well, I was just thinking out loud, I guess. But I'm convinced that there are a few—very few—persons that I have had to deal with in my life that I cannot honestly say 'I like.' Jim is one of them. Call it a personality clash, if you will. But he could get my dander up, if I let him, faster than anybody I know.

"But I know Jim is a good man, a valuable man, so I can only blame something intangible within myself for not really liking him. Because I believe that this undertone of dislike for Jim is unique with me I never allow myself to blame him for it. Furthermore, I don't know how he feels toward me although I am pretty sure this personality clash is not strictly mutual.

"In any event, my point is that I would not be as successful as I am nor have as few worries without Jim's help. There are, no doubt, times when you can't help disliking something about a person, but if you always put the blame for this dislike on yourself, whether you can put the finger on the cause or not, you will find that you can avoid letting so-called personality clashes from hurting your progress and enjoyment in life."

I think my executive friend offers you one of the best ways to cope with the personality clashes in your life. If you are unable to transplant yourself completely out of the circle of contact with such person, follow this three-step technique and your life will be much happier:

1. Double-check your own behavior and emotional attitude towards the person in question, just to make sure the origin of the "clash" is not in your own lap.

2. Keep your contact with this person on a friendly basis, talk him up behind his back (even if you have to search hard to find something good to say about him), and cross his

path only when circumstances make it imperative for you to do so.

3. Make up your mind that he deserves the opportunity to make his way in life, whether you care to admit it or not. Give him every break in your own mind, and try to use him for what he can do for you through his special abilities, just as my executive friend learned to use Jim as his right-hand man, even though the undertone between them ran quite deep.

To control the emotions of the other person in your own behalf, you must get a clear view of the other person's mental picture of yourself. To do this, it is often necessary to examine your attitude towards him from the vantage or disadvantage view of his eyes!

Here are four questions you should stop and ask yourself any time you stand back and weigh your own stock on the other fellow's scales:

1. How much genuine interest do I show in him, his family, his hobbies, or his worries?
2. Do I really show him the courtesy that I should when he is speaking to me, or do I let my mind wander while my head nods constant approval?
3. How much do I offer to help when he outlines a plan of what he wants to do on the job or off it?
4. Do I support his innermost desires enthusiastically?

You will find, by acting positively on each of the foregoing questions, that you can gain a remarkable command over the other person's emotions towards you.

I recall an occasion when the application of a positive answer to Question Four meant a great deal to me as well as to another person. I had been called into a conference about an idea that had been submitted by an associate. This man wanted to get a patent in the worst way.

My first comments were on the discouraging side as I endeavored to explain to the patent attorney what I considered to be a basic technical weakness of the product for its intended use. This attitude brought momentary belligerence from my associate; it appeared as though I were trying to put a roadblock in the way of one of his innermost objectives. As soon as I sensed his reaction, I hastened to clarify my objective. Immediately, I demonstrated how this man's idea could be directed toward an entirely different market from the one he had been emphasizing, and that in this area the idea was not only technically sound, but its economic potential was exciting!

As soon as my associate realized that I was really behind and not against him, his attitude became most respectful and friendly. He eventually got a patent for his idea in the application toward which I had helped to steer it. But I should have been more careful in not making my initial stand so discouraging to him.

A discouraging opinion, viewpoint, or position always is fraught with dangerous consequences and they should be most carefully avoided.

As the story goes, Satan once decided to go out of business. He offered the tools of his trade for sale. He had no hesitancy to sell such tools as hatred, selfishness, and lying, but there was one tool that he refused to sell at any price. It was the one tool that could put him back in business anytime that he might choose to set up shop again. What was this tool that Satan felt was so vital to his business success? It was called "discouragement."

THE INVADING FRAGRANCE OF PERSUASIVE EMOTIONS

I often recall a Chinese friend of mine. When I had befriended him with a gift, he said, "Flowers always leave part of their fragrance in the hands that give them." I believe that it is this fragrance that you have within your power to leave in the hands of all with whom you come into contact. Each person with whom you meet or associate is bristling with sensitive emotional antenna just as your nostrils respond to the fragrance of perfumes which may be present in the air in a few parts per million.

Here are a few guides to help you leave a breath of your own fragrance with people, guides that will help you to control the emotions of the other persons, so that they will not be directed against you but toward you and for your personal pleasure and profit.

1. You can incite a favorable emotional response by an enthusiastic way of speaking, a soft tone of voice, and pleasant mannerisms.
2. Before you approach a person, make up your mind just what kind of emotional response you want to receive from him. Try to feel this response yourself, and you will be astonished how it will return to you in mirror-like fashion from the other person.
3. Destroy all negative emotional symptoms as soon as they make their appearance. When tenseness appears on the scene, inject humor; when disagreement begins to build up, inject agreement, even if on some unrelated point. When an air of failure begins to cloud a situation, inject optimism and, if necessary, invent a silver lining.

Throughout your life and mine, moods and emotions, alternating between extremes, motivate us. Learn to search out the deepest emotions in the heart of each man, woman, and child, emotions that are important to them and demand your respect. Baby them, cultivate them, and apply the wisdom of the Chinese proverbs in all your dealings with people: "Flowers always leave part of their fragrance in the hands that give them."[1]

Human emotions are as contagious as measles: an emotional pattern in one person will breed the same emotional pattern in another just as a mirror instantly reflects your own image.

Learn the priceless value of humor to relieve explosive situations. Nothing will dispel the pressure of a head of steam like hearty laughter.

Remember, too, that your face is a mirror into which the other person constantly is looking, searching out, or sensing his true standing with you.

Apply these five key principles for controlling the emotions of others:

1. Speak only the "good word" about people.
2. Never show disrespect for the religious belief of others.

---

[1] If you feel that your ability to control your emotions in dealing with people is one of your glaring weaknesses, I recommend that you read *Finding and Using Your Magic Emotion Power* by Eugene J. Benge (Englewood Cliffs, N.J.: Prentice-Hall, Inc., 1958).

3. Beware of goring your popularity by being a bore yourself.
4. Don't let perfectionmania give you the stigma of an unpopular holier-than-thou reputation.
5. Never *demand* that your importance be acknowledged by others.

8.

Listen—and Develop a Magnetic Personality

AN OLD UNCLE OF MINE HAD HIS OWN PECULIAR ways. He would spend a great deal of time talking to himself. One day I asked him why he did this and he replied, "Well, there are two reasons why I like to talk to myself. First of all, I like to listen to a smart man talk, and secondly I like to talk to a smart man!" He lived until the age of 99 and was very successful. "I attribute my good health," he told a reporter, "to the fact that, except for brief spells when I've enjoyed talking to myself, I've always listened!"

Some years ago, my immediate superior advised me, "Let the other man talk himself out. Always be willing to listen to someone tell you about his 'fishing' success in life and you never will have to worry about the size of the ones you catch yourself."

FIVE STEPS TO GOOD LISTENING

1. "Sit up" and listen instead of "sitting back" and listening.
2. Show by your face as well as your posture that your mind is alert in addition to your ears being open.

3. Ask questions softly and seldom, and if you can, choose questions you are confident the other person will enjoy answering.
4. When a person talks to you seriously about himself or his accomplishments, lend him more than a sympathetic ear. Encourage him to talk some more and he will think you are brilliant!
5. Make up your mind that at least half of what you listen to is worth remembering. If it isn't, perhaps you had better upgrade the kind of listening you do, if at all possible.

Take time out to go through any organization with which you are familiar. Honestly answer these questions:

1. Who are the people you like the most?
2. Why are certain people welcomed in a crowd with open arms?

Your answer will include unhesitantly those few who always have the interest and patience to hear you out, or to "sit up" and listen. They are the people who leave you or a group with the impression that they enjoy listening more than they do talking. Take a leaf out of your own book of experience and apply it in your dealings with others. A good listener never is accused of being a bore.

I know of few human beings, no matter their station in life, who are immune to the sudden flattery of rapt attention. There is no higher compliment that you can pay a person than the exclusive attention you can give that person simply by listening to him. The royal road to a man's heart is simply to get him to talk to you about what he treasures most or about that which he holds the deepest convictions.

Early in my career as an author and lecturer I was invited to give an address to a large audience in New York City. Over 1000 persons had come to hear me talk about the message upon which my book *How to Enjoy Work and Get More Fun Out of Life* (Englewood Cliffs, N.J.: Prentice-Hall, Inc., 1957) was based. I was flattered and astonished in experiencing the thrill of watching the interested faces of a thousand persons as they listened to me talk! Little did they realize that their listening was many times more satisfying to me than the fee I was to collect for delivering my talk to them.

There is a little man who sits in a big office in the research department of a large corporation outside New York. If you ask him what his job is, his face usually lights up with a smile and he says, "I get paid to listen."

This man's title is that of "Senior Scientist." He does nothing but keep the door to his office (and his ears) open to any and all of the scientists on the research staff who may wish to come in and talk. He is so popular, so much in demand, that his secretary has to line up appointments with him days in advance. At chemical conventions I have heard his associates make such compliments as:

1. "Dr. W. knows more about cellulose chemistry than anybody else in the country. I just love to visit him and tell him about my problems."
2. "There goes a man who can inspire more ideas than the Chase National Bank."
3. "The thing I like most about Dr. W. is that when you discuss a problem with him you always come away with a good idea or two on how to solve it."

Yet the facts are (I know Dr. W. well) that he always is long on the listening and short on the talking. Sometimes, he finds that the person he is listening to gets the solution to his problem as he talks to him about it, and Dr. W. does not have to say a word. There are many well-paid executives in all walks of life like Dr. W. Chances are that each of them, like Dr. W., would tell you in a quiet moment, "I get paid to listen."

And all their friends will go around singing the praises of their truly magnetic personalities.

Practical Benefits of Being A Good Listener

1. You always will be given credit for being more intelligent than you know you are.
2. You will give yourself the kind of education that you cannot possibly get elsewhere.

3. You will acquire an ever-widening circle of friends including many important ones, who will seek you out each time they want a sounding board on which to test their ideas or vent their emotions.
4. You will learn more about others than you could ever guess, because people always end up telling a good listener much more than they ever intended at the start.
5. You will be surprised at the weight of things people will quote you as having said to them simply because they become so deeply moved by your rapt ear-attentiveness.

Four Essential Marks of A Good Listener

1. To be a good listener you must want to listen. This means that you must get completely clear of yourself. If your own personal problems occupy your mind, it is extremely difficult to listen properly to the other person.
2. To be a good listener, you must provide sympathy and silence. Listening is in reality a form of showing affection! Nine times out of ten, the friend or associate who comes to you with the object of soliciting your ears wants affection and reassurance more than anything else.
3. To be a good listener, and to profit from listening, you should take the initiative to provide the proper setting. You must insure privacy when possible in order to give the speaker your undivided attention.
4. To be a good listener you must be a willing sounding board. You can best do this by establishing direct eye-contact with the person speaking to you. You should show by your posture and facial expression that the speaker's problems are a matter of deep concern to you. It would be well always to remember what G. K. Chesterton said, "There is no such thing as an uninteresting subject; there are only uninterested people." If you are willing to make the effort, you can always find something interesting in each person you meet; the effort need be no more burdensome than that of opening your ears and closing your mouth.

George is a very successful business executive that I know.

When he feels that an associate needs his undivided attention he invariably suggests that they go for a drive in his car.

"For one thing," he told me, "we know then that we have absolute privacy. On the other hand, I have something to do that will help me to keep my own mouth shut. I am able to pay attention to my driving without handicapping my listening ability. Furthermore, in such a relaxed atmosphere, the inevitable periods of silence are not nearly so awkward and the scenery along the way is always a good outlet for fill-in-conversation."

George pays great attention to the listening part of his job because he realizes, as do most business executives today, that as much as 50 per cent of his workday (and salary) is directly tied to listening on the job. He also knows that most of his less successful associates listen with only about 25 per cent efficiency!

Listening on the job can be a tremendous asset to you. It can become a rare charm. When you are a good listener your associates, be they day laborers or financiers, lab technicians or corporation vice-presidents, know they can face a man who will surely see eye-to-eye with them. Few comments speak more favorably in behalf of a boss than to hear someone say about him, "He listens," or, "I can talk to him." Such a boss is headed for the top.

On the other hand, when a boss is pegged by such comments as "He knows it all," and, "If I try to tell him he won't listen to me," then somebody is losing ground fast. As Cicero put it almost two thousand years ago, "There is an art in silence, and there is an eloquence in it too." As the late Dorothy Dix in more recent years wrote, "All you need in order to get the reputation of being a fascinating person is to say to the other person, 'How wonderful! Do tell me some more!'"

A well-liked and very effective executive, Jerry, uses his listening ability to great advantage. I recall an instance when he walked into his office, brief case in hand, after being away on an extremely important business trip. Because he had been out of town for almost a week, his desk was swamped with urgent correspondence and pending telephone calls. But he knew that a member of his staff was due back on the job after a gall bladder operation that morning. I was deeply impressed to see Jerry, holding his coat over one hand and brief case in the other, leaning against the desk of the man who had just returned to work, listening eagerly to each detail of the operation and convalescence. Jerry had deliberately gone to see this man—even before checking into his own office because he knew the latter would be primed to tell him his story.

By putting short spurts of his valuable time to work in this way, listening to specific members of his staff especially when he knew they desperately wanted the boss to listen to them, Jerry built up a group who were wholeheartedly devoted to him. Here, indeed, is a man who has found that there is real "gold" in deliberately establishing listening periods.

There is no question about it; whoever you are, whatever you do, wherever you may be on life's success-ladder, the secret of getting along harmoniously, happily and successfully, is to lend people both of your ears at every opportunity. After all, there is nothing you can say to the other person that will be half as interesting to him as what he is dying to tell you about himself.

Some of the most successful people that I know in the sales world, believe it or not, are expert listeners. Frequently they place a key question with a potential customer to make that customer start talking about himself. Then they sit back and listen. They seldom get a chance to talk about themselves and they do this purposely. But when they get ready to leave, and bring up the question of an order, they always walk out with a nice fat one. By letting the customer do the talking, they decrease the chance that they will talk themselves out of a sale.

Howard falls into the class of the listening-type of salesman. "Ever since I talked myself out of the biggest real estate sale of my life, I've become the listening-type salesman. Most customers know exactly what they want from you. Frequently their minds are made up as to how big an order, if any, they will give you, soon after they size you up. If you will sit back and encourage them to talk they can, with a minimum of guidance from you, do a much better job of placing orders on your books than you could ever hope to do by monopolizing the conversation."

Here are several tips that Howard offers on how to use the art of listening effectively to sell yourself or your product to others:

1. Tone down your I's, spruce up the other fellow's.
2. When you ask a question, be sure it does not jar the speaker into a less appealing train of thought for him.
3. When the other fellow has talked himself out, remember that's when he's usually most ready to listen to you.

The secretary to the president of a large American Corporation is paid considerably more than some of the department managers in this company. Why? Because this lady really knows how to listen. She knows that her pay comes from what she does not say rather than from what she does say. Her ability to keep her ears open and her mouth closed, the discretion with which she uses her tongue, are her most valuable assets. This is a most important counterpart of being a successful listener.

One of the problems with being a good listener is that your friends and associates will take you into their innermost confidence. When they do, treasure these confidences with your life or your reputation as a listener will deteriorate like an ice cream cone on a hot sunny day.

To be a good listener, therefore, you must develop a reputation in advance of being a non-gossiper. People who like to gossip may enjoy swapping stories, but they have a hard time getting the really important people in their lives to stop with them much longer than it takes to say "Hello" and "Good-bye."

Someone has quipped, "One of the virtues of being a good listener is that people will think the world of you for it and you don't have to hear a word they say!" Like most quips, however, this is only a half-truth. Pretended listening can be one of the most damaging obstacles in your efforts to influence people.

You may think you are fooling the person who is talking to you by giving him an occasional nod or grunt. But you cannot fool his supersensitive built-in antennae, which can sense even the slightest insincerity on your part. Pretended listening is a grave insult to a speaker, one which he is apt to remember for a very long time.

On the other hand, when a person knows that he has a good listener, he can sense it. He will share his thoughts more fully and, as he talks, the person needing help will sometimes find a good solution to his problems. After all, the most important tool of the modern psychiatrist is the art of sympathetic listening. You will search far and long before you will find a *successful* psychiatrist who can be accused of being a "critical," "boring," or a "pretender" type of listener.

THE TEN MOST COMMON PITFALLS OF A BAD LISTENER

Bad listening, of course, can be like bad manners. The trouble with most of us is that we become rather infatuated with the sound of our voices and act rudely. A bad listener is usually an egotist and a bore. He is a person who is bubbling over with his own importance or who considers himself an authority on every subject that comes up for discussion. A bad listener is a person who talks braggingly out of the corner of his mouth, who possesses too much self-confidence, who becomes pegged among his associates as one of the great "I am's." He is bound to have little or no power to influence people successfully.

Here are ten things that you should take especial care to do in order to develop the art of listening and get along better with people because of it.

1. Be listener-centered instead of self-centered.
2. Try, without bias, to evaluate what the other speaker is saying. Curb negative emotional reactions to what you hear.
3. One of the worst faults of listeners is that they may not like the person who is talking to them. They show it all over their face. Letting your feelings about the person who is talking to you influence your judgment is a very serious violation of the rules of good listening.
4. Never daydream when you are listening. Remember that it is possible for you to listen about four times as fast as a person can speak to you. So always be on guard against letting your mind wander during the other three-fourths of the time.
5. Beware of being the type of listener who sits on edge and

is ready to jump in and provide the answers rather than
to stand by to ask more questions.

6. When the person is speaking to you, do not let your mind
work overtime trying to figure out how you will refute what
he is saying. A good listener shows affection to the speaker,
as well as politeness, kindness, and consideration.

7. While the speaker is talking, by all means never pretend
you are just listening. If you let your mind wander away,
the person speaking to you is the first who will detect it.

8. Beware of setting yourself up as a cynical, unsympathetic
listener by letting your eyes grow cold at the mention of
such things as religion, nationality, or political preference.

9. Do not be a fidgity listener. Appear calm and relaxed. Do
not finger your Phi Beta Kappa key or clean your pipe or
keep twisting in your seat when you are supposed to be
listening to someone.

10. Beware of becoming what you might call an open-mouth
listener, one who must say something each time the
speaker stops to catch his breath.

I know of no more effective anecdote to illustrate the tremendous and far-reaching implications of being a bad listener than
the story offered recently by a newspaper reporter. Two men
came home from work. Each greeted his wife in a different way.
The first man said "Darling, when I look into your face time
stands still." The second man, however, said "My dear, your face
would stop a clock." Yet husband number one got into trouble
because his wife was such a poor listener she misinterpreted her
husband's remark. She thought she heard, "When I look into
your face, I can't stand still!" Husband number two got off scot-
free because his wife also was a poor listener. She thought he had
said, "Your face would make a clock stop to look at you," and
assumed it to be a compliment.

The completely unexpected reactions that came from such
simple statements are illustrative of the repercussions that can
come by being a bad listener. How often in our daily living we
learn of unnecessary arguments and deep animosities being

started just because somebody gets a wrong slant by being a poor listener! All too often a poorly heard compliment is taken to heart as a slap in the face! At other times careless listening can result in physical harm.

That is exactly what happened in an Ohio tire manufacturing plant. Two systems of pressure for molding tires were in use: air, and super-heated steam. An operator who paid insufficient attention to instructions from his foreman "thought" he was told to use steam pressure instead of air pressure to discharge a certain rubber molding. Because he failed to listen attentively, he ended up in a hospital with steam burns all over his face.

Children, even unusually bright children, who are not taught the importance of attentive "listening" by their parents or teachers frequently get inferior grades. In our home we were taught the habit of careful listening by observing silence at dinner time while one member of the family read appropriate selections from current magazines or books which no one else would have had a chance to read earlier.

One of the difficulties of attentive listening stems from the fact that you are able to *think* twice as fast as a person can speak to you. To be a careful listener frequently means you must deliberately slow down your thinking apparatus so that your memory does not get too far ahead of what you are hearing at a particular moment.

An internal medicine specialist told me he spends 75 per cent of his total working time listening carefully to patients' thoughts. "I find," he told me, "that the best clues to a patient's problem often begin exposing themselves after I let them talk for ten minutes. If it is a really tough case, I usually let him know that I want to listen to what he has to say for still another ten minutes!"

The surest way to convince the other fellow in the long run that you are one of the wisest, most intelligent persons he has ever met is simply by paying attention to what he has to say. It was Justice Oliver Wendell Holmes who wrote, "To be able to listen to the other person in a sympathetic and understanding manner is perhaps the most effective mechanism in getting along with people and tying up their friendship for good. Too few people practice the *white magic of being good listeners."*

Key Things a Speaker Looks for in a Listener

1. A speaker's main interest, whether he's talking to one or a thousand persons, is his audience. He is constantly sizing you up, analyzing your innermost reactions to his words, and weighing you on a delicate balance of his own emotions. Make sure you present yourself as a friendly audience to him.

2. First, last, and always, his paramount interests lie with his job, his family, and his ideas; he is seeking your ears to secure your approval of them.

3. He seeks trustworthiness in you as a sounding board, often in order to make his speech or conversation a safe means for letting off steam. As a listener, when you know you are being so used, you can make a friend for life by showing understanding, patience, and extended silence.

4. He enjoys talking to you only as long as he is sure you are enjoying listening to him. Show him that this is so and he will build you up as a wonderful, even brilliant, person behind your back.

5. He expects *you* to benefit from what he tells you. If you are a good listener, and pick the right persons to whom to listen, you will be astonished at how much you can learn this way.

Some of the greatest men who ever lived were especially good listeners. They knew that by listening to what a man told them, by understanding exactly how a situation affected that man, they could actually spark that man's enthusiasm for them.

The great military successes of Dwight D. Eisenhower are known to have been based on the fact that he always listened to the advice of his subordinates and weighed it carefully in reaching his own decisions. This is true of almost every great leader; he gathers around him people of integrity and intellectual ability, people who are really worth hearing. Calvin Coolidge, for example, was called Northampton's champion listener. Such men as Andrew Carnegie, Charles Schwab, Henry Ford, and a great many others were great listeners. Eventually they also became great men to whom it was certainly worth listening.

A leading authority in the art of good oral communication, Dr. William Hillary, told me recently that noise, vocal noise, is the most serious problem in establishing good oral understanding.

"Your life would be longer, richer, more fruitful" comments Dr. Hillary, "if you will only spend a greater share of it in the tranquility of meditative listening. We are such a noisy lot that most of what we say goes unheard and unheeded. We are in the 'Stone Age' still when it comes to using the wonders of our tongue and our ears in our own best interest and for the good of our fellow men. Listening, I would say, is the finest art still to be mastered by man."

More persons can prove that their success stems more from listening than from talking.

Nothing will make you a "greater guy" than giving others a chance to talk themselves out. Listening is one of the most appreciated forms of flattery.

Avoid these three marks of a bad listener that can prevent you from ever becoming the "brilliant" fellow you may hope to be:

1. Never be a critical listener. Show the other person you enjoy the fact that he has the floor.
2. Beware of interjecting the sound of your own voice.
3. "Pretended listening" is worse than a refusal to listen at all! Nothing will arouse resentment toward you like an obvious revelation that you are lending only one ear to what is being said.

Once again, use the following five steps to develop your power to influence people through the art of listening:

1. "Sit up" and listen; do not simply "sit back" while listening.
2. Show by your face as well as your posture that your mind, as well as your ears, is open and alert.
3. Ask questions softly and seldom, and, as well as you can, choose questions the other person will enjoy answering.

4. When a person talks to you seriously about himself or his accomplishments, lend him more than a sympathetic ear; encourage him to talk some more and he will think you are brilliant!

5. Try to remember the essentials of what you receive in listening.

9.

Letters: Vital Cogs in the Wheel of Human Relations

WHEN IT COMES TO WINNING THE FRIENDSHIP and support of some of the most influential people, a single letter can assume crucial importance. The battle for success often is more than half won whenever you are able to get into personal contact with key persons who can influence your career most favorably. Many times such introductions are impossible through the normal channel of a personal introduction. Time and time again, however, the use of a single letter may be the magic key opening your door to a contact that will set you on course for the rest of your life.

I have before me a letter from the president of one of the largest men's service organizations in the world. It begins as follows: "With warm appreciation, I acknowledge receipt of your cordial and thoughtful letter. It made my whole day brighter." Some weeks after I had received this letter, I had occasion to want to interview this gentleman in connection with a magazine article I was doing. To oblige me he went out of his way to the point of cancelling a previously scheduled conference. Without my original letter, in which I commented upon a television speech he had made, the chances are I would have received the routine no-go treatment. As it turned out, he gave me two hours of his time and took me to lunch on top of that. And the article proved to be one of my most successful "profile" pieces in years.

While preparing to write the book *How to Enjoy Work and Get More Fun Out of Life* (Englewood Cliffs, N.J.: Prentice-Hall, Inc., 1957), I was astounded at the wonderful interest and cooperation which 18 of America's outstanding leaders gave me. Such men as Harlow H. Curtice, Henry Ford II, General David Sarnoff, and the late Charles F. Kettering shared their time and talents freely with me. Yet my initial contact with each of these great Americans did not come about through a personal introduction by one of his close friends or business associates; I introduced myself to him by means of a first-class letter, a truly magic messenger that is capable of breaking through a barrier of six front-office secretaries.

Key business and personal friends of yours, as well as celebrities with a national reputation, are constantly wondering where they stand with the rest of the world. In this respect they are human just as you are; but they usually are far more sensitive about it! They know that *others* can put their finger on the pulse of their reputation better than they can do so themselves.

Irving Hoffman, the Broadway wit and columnist, like many others in his competitive profession, has used little notes and letters to become a close friend of some of the most famous people in the world. His technique, a perfectly valid one for you to apply as the circumstances may permit, was to mail to these celebrities unusual statements that he heard about them in the course of his contacts or travels.

Letters can be especially useful in overcoming the greatest handicap most of us have, that of not getting to know people because of the fear of rejection. A short, friendly letter is the first course, so to speak, in such an ordeal. So often, through purposeful and well-written letters of introduction, you can come to know the man at the top and find it far easier to deal with him in an informal way than do some of his closest associates.

Here are sample letters that you might find useful for "breaking the ice" under appropriate circumstances, as well as to help you become a more effective letter-writer:

Case 1: Making a First Contact with a Topflight Businessman or Celebrity to Request a Favor

Before writing such a letter, be sure to go to the trouble of getting vital statistics about the person. Reference books with such information are available at any public library. If the person has a Ph.D., an O.B.E., or some other distinction, you can tell him in advance of a direct personal interview, by recognition of this honor in your first contact through correspondence, that you *are* familiar with his or her past record.

Let us suppose you are program chairman for an important meeting and want to get a prominent businessman to be the principal speaker. A letter like the following might bring you success with your assignment:

Dear Mr. X:

I read recently a copy of a speech you gave before a meeting of business analysts in New York City. It was passed on to me by an employee of your company.

With the wholehearted approval and unanimous interest of the directors of our organization, it is with genuine pleasure that I extend to you an invitation to address our membership at its annual husband-and-wife dinner meeting on ———.

We know that each of us will be better Americans and be better able to handle our civic and community obligations as a result of listening to the deeply significant message you could give us.

We are extremely hopeful, Mr. X, that you will afford the five hundred members of our organization the privilege of hearing you in person by accepting this invitation which I am most happy to extend to you in their behalf.

Yours most sincerely,

John Doe

Program Chairman

Notes About Case I

1. The opening paragraph combines a light touch of flattery with a firm touch of fact.
2. The second paragraph lends weight to the invitation, so that it does not appear routine.
3. The third paragraph calls on the nobler sentiments of the man.
4. Paragraph four uses an effective style—the use of the man's name once, and only once, in the body of the letter. It also closes the letter on a note that makes it so easy for your request to be granted.

Case II. Making Contact With a Business Firm to Introduce a New Product or Service

Before writing such a letter, find out the correct person in the organization to whom your letter should be addressed. With relatively small companies, you can usually get this person's name and official company title by a telephone call to the receptionist, telling her of your interests and asking her guidance to the man's name you are seeking. Telephone operators and receptionists usually are flattered to receive such bona fide requests and almost always are fully cooperative. If the organization is a very big corporation, you might get to the correct party by contacting an employee you know, or going directly to the Director of Research and Development. When in doubt, however, the best procedure is to address your letter to the top man, the president, checking ahead of time to be sure that you have the right name and office location. When the president of a company pencils a notation on such a letter, it means it impressed him favorably, and that the man to whom he routes it is the right man to deal with. The fact that your initial contact reached him by route of the company's president will not detract in the least from the consideration you will receive; it may well increase it.

Dear Mr. Y:

We have just developed a new product that our tests show could improve the whitening action of your laundry bleach. Our product is called XYZ. It is only 50 cents a pound in quantity lots, yet our data show that as little as 2 percent added to a laundry bleach such as your excellent Z-X increases its bleaching effectiveness by almost 60 percent.

If you will let me know when it would be convenient for you to have me visit you to demonstrate this significant new product and, if you so desire, review our results with members of your technical staff, I will be glad to make my visit as worthwhile to your company as possible.

Very truly yours,

John Doe, Manager
New Product Development

Notes About Case II:

1. You clearly show that you are interested in improving your contact's products to his advantage; so far as his business interests are concerned nothing interests him more.
2. You can show you are not talking through your teeth, that you are willing to prove you have a product that will mean "money in the bank" for him.
3. You make it easy, without any risk to him, for your contact to hear your story out.
4. You said your piece, and stopped! This is the best possible way to make your contact say *to himself,* as you hoped he would, "We better see this fellow or our competitors might get a head start on us."

Typical Do's and Don'ts of Letter-Writing

Over the years I have collected good and bad phrases in personal and business letters that have crossed my desk. I have compiled a list of the most common "Don'ts" together with my suggestions for substitutions. You may find this list increasingly useful to you with your future letter writing chores. Underlying the substitutions are two themes: emphasis on the editorial "We," and the use of brief and popular (not old-fashioned) business English.

LETTER-WRITING "DON'TS"	SUGGESTED SUBSTITUTES
(a) I; me; mine, the undersigned	We; us; ours, I
(b) —acknowledge arrival of yours of 2nd instant	In reply to your letter of June 2
(c) Attached hereto you will find	Attached is
(d) In accordance with your kind request	At your request
(e) At this writing	Today
(f) Pursuant to our telephone conversation yesterday	As agreed on the telephone yesterday
(g) Please be advised	We are happy to tell you
(h) You may rest assured	We can say

Outdated letter-writing phrases that are best omitted completely:

> in reference to
> in connection with
> regret to advise
> take the liberty of
> meets with your approval
> I remain or I am
> Your letter has come to hand

The Importance of the Personal Touch in Letters

I know of no better way to tell someone to whom you may be indebted "I like you," "I respect you," "I value your friendship," or, "I enjoy being of help to you," than through the courtesy of a handwritten note.

One day when I was in the office of the president of a large publishing company, I observed him signing the day's dictation. What impressed me was the number of personal P.S. notes which he added to perfectly typed correspondence as he signed his mail. The success and influence of this publisher puts him close to the top, if not at the top in his field. I do not think it is overstating the point to say that his friendly handwritten comments in the margins or as postscripts in his letters have gone a long way toward making him as successful as he is with contacts in almost every country in the world.

This publisher was following a practice which President Theodore Roosevelt also used frequently. "Teddy" Roosevelt never hesitated to upset his meticulous private secretary by inking in an added thought or two on the margins of a perfectly typed letter.

The writing of a "Thank you" letter is one of the most delicate and yet most effective ways to make yourself appreciated by others. Frequently, however, it is a good idea in writing a "Thank you" note to avoid expressing excessive appreciation for an obvious courtesy, act of thoughtfulness, or warm consideration shown to you.

At one time we entertained a couple at our home for a weekend. We had entertained them on several occasions before. But on this particular weekend we decided to treat them to something special and out of the ordinary. It was Easter time. The beautiful spring flowers at the famous DuPont Longwood Gardens in Delaware were at the peak of their hothouse beauty and we treated them to a tour of these magnificent indoor flower gardens.

When we received their "thank you" letter some days later (they were from Minnesota), it was especially heart-warming for us to read it. They were grateful in their note for the usual hospitality that we extended to them, of course. But the real warmth of their note was for the memories they gained for having seen, at the end of a hard, bleak winter, such a thrilling glimpse of mother nature at her spring-best several weeks ahead of normal schedule.

DEVELOP THE "IDEA-LETTER" HABIT

Idea-Letter to Collect That Loan

There is no end of wonderful opportunities for you if you will originate idea-letters that can improve your business or station in life. One man I know, the manager of the credit department of a large department store, is constantly figuring out new ways of building better relationships with customers through the mails. For example, when someone is overdue with the payment on a bill, he sends them a personal letter like this:

"We want to let you know how much we have appreciated the regular manner in which you have always paid your account. We are glad to have customers like you and can promise you every consideration and service in order to keep you as our customer. If, for any reason, your overdue account cannot be paid now, perhaps you would give us the opportunity of sharing your problem with you so that we may continue our pleasant and understanding friendship in the future."

Idea-Letter to Contact Your Future Boss

One time writing an appropriate letter can mean a great deal to a person is immediately after a company appoints him to a top managerial post or other position of great responsibility. This is especially true when such an announcement is made in connection with a shake-up, a general house-cleaning within a company.

The case of a young man I know, who emerged on top from one of those "volcanic" eruptions within a Chicago metal products firm, is worth telling about.

Some days after the new vice-president had had an opportunity to learn his new job, and meet most of the people who were going to be responsible to him, this young man wrote to him. Not only did he wish the man well, but he explained how he felt his particular background and experience might be an asset to the former's new organization when he established it more firmly. He enclosed a resume of his previous experience along with his assurance that he would do everything possible to help the new vice-president put fresh life into his reorganized department. It is more than a coincidence or "a lucky break" on the part of the young man that he happens to be a Special Assistant reporting directly to this vice-president.

Idea-Letter to Arrange a First Interview

A first interview with some important person in your life is much easier to arrange by the proper type of letter-writing in advance. In some cases I have waited years, after repeated exchanges of correspondence, before tactfully suggesting a personal interview with a prominent person. Invariably such interviews are then granted. I dare say if they had been requested at the time of my first correspondence they would have been rejected. With letter-writing, it is sometimes more important to use the proper *timing* than it is to use the proper *wording*.

Take Henry's case, which lead to an equally successful result. He was a young executive employed by a mammoth chemical company. The son of the president of a different company, after graduating from college, was assigned the task of working with Henry. As an apprentice to a man like Henry, this young man would soon learn the business from the ground up. At the end of nine months' association with this unassuming and hard-working young man, Henry decided to write a personal letter to his parents.

In that letter, confidential as it was, he told the president of the company and his wife of the great pleasure that he had had working with their son. He pointed out to them that he admired their son's modesty, his consistent good judgment, his conscientiousness and his technical ability. He further emphasized that never in a single instance did their son say anything or do anything which would reflect any effort on his part to capitalize on his father's prestige and importance.

Henry received the most heart-warming and appreciative reply. His letter had provided the young man's father with precisely the information he was seeking, but which he was almost helpless to obtain in an unbiased manner.

Henry's letter and the unsolicited consideration it revealed about him remained headlined in this president's mind for years. It was perfectly timed, and it registered itself indelibly in a warm spot within the heart of an important man in Henry's life. Later, a long time later, it was to become the key which would open opportunity's door for Henry. Eventually Henry was offered (and he accepted) a top managerial post in the company headed by the father of the young man he had coached. Today he is a vice-president of this company and a member of the board of directors.

THE POWER OF CONSTRUCTIVE LETTERS

When Walter S. Franklin was president of the Pennsylvania Railroad, I wrote him at length explaining my displeasure, and the harmful repercussions to his company, of the five- and even ten-minute delays in trying to make a telephone contact with the reservation desk at the 30th Street Station in Philadelphia. I received a personal reply of appreciation from Mr. Franklin, but he went even further. He dispatched an assistant to visit with me at my residence to discuss at length with me this weakness in their service.

The answer to the problem became clear to them as soon as they made a detailed study of it after I called it to their attention in a constructive, not belligerent, spirit. There were a couple times during each day, it was found, when reservation requests reached such great numbers that their staff was inadequate to handle them; on the other hand, during the rest of the workday their existing staff was more than adequate.

As a result they did some rejuggling and improved the reservations service during the peak periods. As a matter of fact, today, instead of an unending busy signal, a prompt response and even a courteous "I'll be with you in a moment, sir," if no one is immediately available to take your request, comes through.

In my files is a letter from the Commissioner of Pennsylvania's State Police telling me that he has instructed engineers to correct a hazardous intersection on a highway north of Media, Pennsylvania: stop lights would be installed promptly. A survey of the intersection, brought about by a letter from me, definitely showed that action in the interests of safety was warranted. He felt my letter helped him do a better job. I wrote it only in the hope of heading off certain death for motorists at some future date if visibility at the busy intersection were not improved and a traffic light not installed. Imagine the wonderful chance of saving lives through a four-cent stamp!

A good friend of mine and a very successful insurance company executive, Bill Leighton, taught me how to use a telegram or a special delivery letter in the most effective way. Some years ago I was awarded a doctorate. Upon returning to my hotel room I found a telegram awaiting me. When I opened it, I was warmly impressed to read:

"Congratulations!—Bill Leighton."

Ever since, I have used this one-word bouquet on many deserving friends and associates, but I generally send it on in the form of an air mail special delivery letter. I know that the recipients of these one-word letters have appreciated them as I did mine.

When persons you know, even remotely, win a big promotion, perform a great community task, or inherit a million dollars, dispatch a letter to them promptly. You would be surprised at how few bouquets these persons ever receive in the mail, and the number of years later that they will remember your bouquet!

There is something unique about a letter handwritten under unusual circumstances that proves the sincerity, interest, or thoughtfulness of the sender. For example, I have such a letter from Sidney D. Kirkpatrick, Vice-president of McGraw-Hill Publishing Company. It is a delightful complimentary note written in his own handwriting immediately after reading a chapter in my book *How to Enjoy Work and Get More Fun Out of Life*. Dr. Kirkpatrick wrote to say he wanted to reprint this chapter in one of his magazines, *Chemical Engineering*, because he thought it would fit in so well with the "You and Your Job" department in the magazine. The interesting thing about this letter was the notation at the beginning of it which is as follows:

> Enroute to Los Angeles,
> Aboard United DC-7,
> 23,000 feet.

The late Merle Crowell, as a Senior Editor at *The Reader's Digest*, probably did more to steer me into a successful writing career than any other person. And he did it through dozens of letters in which he patiently tore apart drafts of articles I had offered him. I recall vividly his first "helpful" letter received many years ago because it did so much to glue my feet to the ground, where they belonged.

"You must have had a good time writing 'And Sudden Blindness,'" he wrote. "Quite an array of verbal lushness, elastic imagery, prose-poetry! You probably sat back and read it over and over. Then you said, 'That's really good.' Then you read it again and shipped it to me posthaste in the belief that it was a masterpiece. Sorry, but I'm throwing it back at you. Now, write me an article packed with lively and interesting fact and anecdote, simply told, and see how nice I can be."

I wrote Mr. Crowell of my genuine appreciation of his criticism. This was proof enough to him that I was serious about this writing business, that I was willing to *use criticism* to improve myelf. As a result, Merle Crowell wrote to me steadily over the years helping me in no small way to sell to the slick magazines. I believe a text on journalism could be written based entirely upon the letters he sent me.

When I was a single man, I developed a crush on a pretty little "Pennsylvania Dutch" girl from Reading. Despite my efforts to interest her in me, I did not seem to be making much headway.

One day I helped an elderly man fix a flat tire on his car along a roadside. He noticed that I seemed downhearted. As we worked away, he asked me what was troubling me. I told him the pretty girl I was crazy about never even bothered to answer my letters. "I doubt if she even reads them," I told him.

"Tell you what, son" he smiled. "You've been kind to me, and I'm going to let you in on an idea. Buy yourself some linen cloth paper, the kind that takes a he-man to tear up. Then you write a letter to your sweety on this and see what happens. Good luck!"

I followed his advice. And behold! I received a reply by return mail. "I read your letter and tried to tear it up like I did the others after I read them, but this time I couldn't! Your persistence intrigues me. Yes, I'll accept your invitation for next Saturday night."

The little blonde girl from Reading, Pennsylvania, is now Mrs. Battista.

I tell this personal story because it does illustrate a few of the most important points about using letters to achieve your goals in life:

1. When you write a letter, remember that its purpose is to get an active response from the recipient.

2. Know in advance what you want this response to be, even if it is so simple a response as wanting the other person to like you better.
3. And, most important of all, persevere and make it as difficult as possible for the person who gets the letter to tear it up before reading it.

10.

Tact—The Golden Key to Influencing Others

TACT, WHEN PROPERLY APPLIED, CAN BRING YOU an incredible degree of prestige and poise. It is a golden masterkey to personal happiness, and to power and success with people. If you make every word, act, or gesture a tactful one, the results will amaze and astonish you. The good influence of your use of tact will spread like rippling waves along your route in life. It can be life's best release for tension in your daily contacts with others. It is like a governor for the human machine, a control whereby you acquire a conciliatory reputation and a valuable capacity to understand others and their problems.

There once was a little boy, so the story goes, who lived with his mother high in the Italian Alps.

One day this little boy was punished severely and he shouted at his mother, "I hate you, I hate you, I hate you." As he ran away from home he came to a cliff overlooking a valley. Once again, he cried out, "I hate you, I hate you, I hate you." But when this young boy heard the echo of these words resounding in his ear,

139

he was startled! They sounded mean and distasteful when they came back to his own ears exactly as he had uttered them. The lad was frightened and immediately ran home to his mother. He told her about the bad man in the mountains, the man who had shouted at him, "I hate you, I hate you, I hate you."

The mother took her son back to the mountain. When she arrived at the point where he claimed he had heard the bad man speaking so angrily she said to him, "Now, son, cry out, I love you, I love you, I love you." As soon as he did this, the echo came back clearly, sweetly, "I love you, I love you, I love you."

"That, my son," his mother told him understandingly, "is the law of life: what we give we get back in return."

THE MAGIC POWER OF TACT IN HUMAN RELATIONS

In my own examination of life, I have concluded that the best way to learn to value tact, its magic charms, its great power over the behavior of others, is simply to study the mountains of misery that the tactless people in the world around you bring upon themselves.

Tact, on the other hand, has the magic power of making you uniformly considerate of others, regardless of their station in life or their wealth. It assists in obtaining and maintaining friendly and influential relationships. It prompts you to act with courtesy, diplomacy, genuine appreciation and conscientiousness at all times. Its secret ingredient is the consideration of others. That is why it is the most attractive mark of personality, why it can disarm opponents, liquidate enemies, quiet tempers, calm nerves, and show you the easy way out of difficult and trying situations.

In a nutshell, *tact is the ability that will permit you to give others a shot in the arm as needed without letting them feel the needle.*

Most of the $80,000 a year, which Ed, a corporation executive, earns is paid to him because of his effective use of tact. As the vice-president responsible for some 400 scientists (most of whom are by nature sensitive, even temperamental!), his job literally rests on his ability to get a satisfactory return for his company out of the $7,000,000 a year that it takes to keep such a large corps of technical specialists productive and happy.

Ed is a master at saying "No" without making it sound like "No, No, No!" even when it comes to giving a scientist a performance review without a salary increase. As a matter of fact, it has been said that he can "rake a man over the coals" so tactfully that he sends him back to his laboratory happy and agreeable! Anyone who has had to deal with people in the matter of performance reviews and salary increases knows how difficult a job this is.

Ed does it by combining honesty and frankness with his tact. For example, he might tell an employee: "You've done a good job, John, during the past year, but it was just a good job. Now last year, I gave you a raise on the basis of an outstanding job and, as I've told everybody who works for me, a merit raise in my books is reserved for better-than-good effort. I know you have what it takes to get more salary. So why don't you see what you can do in the next six months to measure up to your best performance. Get on the job more punctually, write your reports without having to be prodded a couple of times, and translate your ideas into practice more quickly. Do these few things and I am sure I can have better news salary-wise the next time we sit down to discuss performance."

Compare Ed with a tactless "boss" a friend once told me about, a Mr. W. It seems that Mr. W. must have been a sadist at heart, and it was only family pull that allowed him to get away with what he did. If a man was normally supposed to have his performance review with Mr. W. in October, he would wait until the end of October before telling the employee, "Your paycheck didn't have an increase in it because your performance the past year didn't qualify you for one. And unless you get on the job on time and spend more time at your lab bench instead of at your desk reading magazines, you won't get a raise next year either—if you're still with us!"

The subtle art of applying tact is to sit down and take council with the person with whom you disagree. It is only by understanding why we differ with each other that the point at issue can ever be resolved. When you fight a person you never find satisfaction. It is only when you yield without violating your basic principles that you get more than you expected.

I once knew a man in a post office who always exhibited a sour facial disposition, a negative attitude toward everybody. I likened him to a porcupine. He did his job with bristles showing from his shoulder. I resolved to see if, through the subtle use of tact, I could get this man, Leo, to smile and be pleasant.

In response to a cheerful "Good morning!" I got a grunt that was hardly audible, and the expression on Leo's face was as sour as a pickle. My next comment made some headway, however. "Leo," I said, "I understand that you know the postal regulations inside out. I have a tough question and no doubt you can help me. I want to mail a book to Canada by parcel post, book rate, and would like to attach a first-class letter to the package. Can I do it?"

I was astonished! Leo's eyes lighted up. "Technically speaking," Leo told me (and I could hardly believe what I heard), "the postal regulations do not allow you to attach a first-class letter to a package going to Canada at the book rate. This privilege—incidentally, the first-class letter can be inside the package as long as you pay its postage and state on the outside of the package that it is inside—applies only to the United States and its territories." But that was not all. Leo continued to post me about many more of the postal regulations that are of special interest to an author. He even opened up to the extent of ending our conversation with "I read and enjoyed your latest book!"

The use of a little tact has worked wonders in my relations with Leo. He now smiles when I speak to him, and yet people in line ahead of me who treat him as bluntly as he treats them still get the gruff, sour treatment for which Leo has become unpopularly known.

How to Criticize and Still Influence People Through Tact

Actually, many men who would not dream of speaking sharply to a secretary or a fellow employee think nothing of barking critically at their wives, children or relatives. It is an enigma of human nature that so many people shower all their sweetness on strangers and abuse their loved ones with their sourness and critical attitudes.

One leading industrialist says that it took him almost 25 years to learn the resounding repercussions of futile criticism. He told me that human beings basically are not creatures of logic but creatures of emotion. Whether they show it on the surface or not, most human beings are enveloped with pride and vanity. They are likely to be super-critical of anything unflattering about their abilities or performance.

"The average person," this executive told me, reacts to criticism or bluntness like a rocket. Bluntness is destructive and almost always valueless. Never criticise unless it is absolutely necessary, and when you do always restrict your criticism to one point, defect, or problem at a time."

If you begin by talking about your own mistakes before you bring up the other fellow's, the chances are you will succeed in correcting the other fellow's errors as well as a few of your own.

One man I know likes to use the statement "I may be wrong, and I frequently am, but let's examine all the facts together." Talk always about your own short-comings before you start to point out the other fellow's. The old saying, "He who treads softly goes far," is very true concerning the road to popularity. The greatest asset you can develop is the ability to show others appreciation and encouragement. Anything you ever do to criticize another person means you are driving a nail into the growth potential of your own future and placing a roadblock in the path to making your own dreams come true.

Here are a few examples selected at random that illustrate how tact can make delicate or bitter situations pleasant and peaceful for all concerned:

1. The shoe clerk says to a lady, who asks which of her feet is larger, "Your left foot is smaller."
2. The personnel manager tells an applicant he is "not young enough" to qualify for a position instead of telling him he is "too old for the job."
3. The girl applies for a job as a model and gets the verdict,

"not slender enough," instead of, "Your legs are too fat."

4. The housewife tells friends, "John isn't too handy with a hammer and saw," instead of, "John is the clumsiest carpenter in the world."
5. The teacher tells a parent, "Your child needs special help in this area," instead of saying, "Frank is a dunce."

The use of tact in a delicate situation is, perhaps, especially best exemplified by the gallant French immigration official charged with filling out a passport for a lady who unfortunately had only one eye. On the passport he wrote: "Eyes brilliant, brown and expressive—only one missing."

Should you ever be driven to criticize someone, hesitate long enough to ask yourself these questions before you plunge ahead:

1. Is there a smile on my face, and in my heart?
2. Am I sure of my facts?
3. Will our talk be in private?
4. Have I considered ways of making my point without unnecessary bluntness?
5. Do I have a compliment to give before I start?

A friend of mine has followed a good rule most successfully for years. "Before I administer criticism, I take the time to criticize myself. Only after I am sure of the approach, even the exact wording, that would impress and help me if I were on the receiving end, do I ever permit myself to deal out criticism to somebody else. This policy has astonished me by the number of times it eliminates the justification for any criticism at all."

Very often it is just the way a thing is said that determines whether you will win a person's cooperation or invite a person's antagonism. Frequently when two people quarrel they do so because one of them said something which the other person interprets differently from the way it was intended. The main requirement in the use of tact, therefore, is to frame your requests so that they will make a "yes" easy and clearly recognized and a "no" painless.

The Phoenicians often used parables to teach moral principles to their children. Parents told their youngsters: "Life is like a magic vase filled to the brim. When you dip into it or draw from it, it overflows into the hands of those who drop treasures into it.

Drop in kindness and you will receive understanding.

Drop in charity and you will receive love.

Drop in hate and you will receive malice.

Drop in envy and you will receive criticism.

You alone control the treasures that life overflows into your heart and hands. Watch carefully what you put into this magic vase."

And the ancient Romans had a wise epigram: "Say nothing but good about the dead." Should not this advice be even more applicable to the living? A dead person cannot be hurt by words; it is only living people who can be hurt by words. After all, life on this whirling planet is much too short to waste time kicking others; besides, your neighbor's boot may be sharper and more painful to bear than your own. There are too many squeaking wheels in this world of ours as it is. You should try to be different: spread soothing words, pour oil on painful wounds, and pull stones out of the other fellow's pasture.

Here are a few key phrases you can use to put tact to work in your behalf.

1. To your wife: "Darling, one of the nicest things you ever did for me was to go over my suits and tighten loose buttons and replace broken ones—without me even asking you! Thoughtfulness like this is what proves that our love is as solid as ever."

2. To a waitress: "I love onion soup, but I'm sorry it doesn't sit well with me. You'd make me happy if I could get clam chowder instead!"

3. To your barber: "Please be kind to those few hairs that are holding out on my forehead. I'm trying to keep my hairline as close to my eyebrows as possible."

4. To your priest, minister or rabbi who has the habit of using big words and making long, boring sermons: "The kind of sermon you do best for me is the kind in which you express profound thoughts in simple words and in less than ten minutes."

5. To a fellow worker: "Let's solve this problem together."
6. To your daughter who insists on wearing your shirt and blue jeans: "I can't wait to see your first formal gown."

EIGHT PRACTICAL WAYS TO USE TACT
IN EVERYDAY LIFE

1. The Tactful Way to Start a Conversation With a Stranger

Jim is one of those persons who can strike up a conversation with anybody as easily as he can light a cigarette with a match. I have studied him for years because there have been times, I must admit—on sitting down beside someone on a diner or airplane, at cocktail parties, even while mingling with a group before giving a lecture—when I felt that I could have used some of Jim's smooth conversation-starting ability.

Here is a list of Jim's most common conversation-openers. You will note in each the subtle tact with which Jim immediately brings the person with whom he wants to meet or talk into the act:

1. I'm very interested in all types of business activities. Would you tell me something about your position and the work you do?
2. I've never seen such attractive cuff links. Could you tell me where I may purchase a pair like them?
3. I'm looking for Dr. Howard Ferguson. I was told he would be here this evening. Could you by any chance point him out to me?
4. Isn't it perfectly delightful to attend a party at the Joneses'? They are such a wonderful couple.
5. Your name fascinates me. Won't you tell me a little about its origin and meaning?
6. How do you manage to go through life and keep such a calm, refreshing composure about yourself?
7. I've never yet met a clergyman of any faith I didn't enjoy talking to. May I get to know you?
8. Have you encountered some of the problems that come with sending a daughter to college these days?

2. The Tactful Way to Ask for a Raise or a Promotion

How you go about asking for a raise and the timing you use can sometimes make the difference between having a job or not, let alone getting a salary increase.

Your supervisor, who is charged by management to recommend a salary increase for you, is sensitive about being told by you that you are way overdue for a raise. Yet, you may be quite justified in prodding him to action; the trouble comes when you try to "railroad" him into action. For this reason, when it comes to asking for and actually getting a raise, tact can really make the difference.

Bill, an accountant I knew, should have known better. But he was hurt because, at a regular performance review, his boss did not say anything to him about a salary increase even though he praised his performance. After mulling the matter over for a few days, Bill became upset; he still felt that he had not received a raise he had earned. He finally decided to act, but unfortunately without tact. He arranged an interview with his supervisor's boss with the idea that he was going to put his cards on the table.

The "Big Boss" listened to Bill's case while Bill orated to him in a "martyred" way. Then he very calmly disciplined Bill in this way:

"I'm sorry to see you take the blunt stand you have taken," the big boss told Bill. " I would never have thought this of you. Your supervisor erred in not explaining to you that we were holding a salary increase up for a month or two because we could see a promotion coming up in that time. Since it is our policy not to give a man a promotion without an appropriate salary increase, I decided to wait so that your raise would be coincident with the promotion and it would be more substantial.

"But Bill, the job we had in mind for you is one that will require the utmost of confidence in your supervisor. It will require the deliberate use of tact in your dealings with people. I realize your mistake in 'jumping the gun' in this instance is a natural and honest one. By all means learn a lesson from it and exercise greater faith and confidence in us in the future."

Compare Bill's *faux pas* with Henry's subtle use of tact to get the raise he felt he deserved. He, too, felt he deserved more money and he got it. He asked for a meeting with his boss's boss, too. But he cleared his request for the interview with his immediate supervisor; he actually arranged the meeting with the "big boss" *through* his supervisor.

"I'm trying hard not to overrate my worth," Henry told the big boss. "But my honest feeling is that I'm about due for more money. If I'm wrong about this I hope you will tell me why and I'll be happy to accept the facts as you may call them." Henry then elaborated on a few of the facts of his performance which he felt were well above the normal call of duty. He even had figures showing in black and white that his suggestions had saved the company several thousands of dollars during the past year.

"I'd like to reopen the matter with your supervisor," the big boss told Henry. "Maybe we have not weighed your performance as accurately as it stacks up in the light of what you say." Henry got his raise, and a big one, too, by applying the soothing salve of tact.

3. The Tactful Way to Turn Down a Request for a Raise

The problem of how to handle a person who wants a raise but doesn't deserve one is constantly faced by supervisors. How it is handled can determine the *esprit de corps* of an organization. Nothing will peg a supervisor in the eyes of management more quickly than his successful handling of the inevitable "raise-by-pass" decision.

Here, indeed, is a problem requiring the ultimate in the use of tact. Gerald is especially successful with such problems. For example, he usually follows this approach: "I can understand your feeling about a raise, Bill, but the only way we can swing it is to make you even more valuable to the company. Now let's break this thing down together and develop a frank plan of action on your part which if you can execute, will certainly make you valuable enough to command a raise say six months or, at most, a year from now." He follows this with a straight-from-the-shoulder listing of Bill's weaknesses and suggests in specific terms how he might immediately proceed to correct them.

The successful leader knows so well the value of preparing a candidate for criticism with a word of praise. You may call this "sugar-coating the pill," but it still makes good sense. After all, the man who made the most money with modern medicines is not the man who developed the pill, but the one who invented the idea of sugar-coating it.

4. The Way to Make Compliments More Effective

A magic wand for the use of tact can be the effective compliment. Compliments, all too often, are so badly made that they boomerang!

A neighbor of ours has such a genuine interest in people that he has hundreds of close friends. "I believe in telling people I like them right to their face—if I really do, that is," he said. "I never had many compliments when I was a boy because my parents seemed to feel that if they praised me it might go to my head. As a result, I felt inferior, unwanted. Because I know from personal experience how starved people are for praise, I speak right out when I like something about someone."

If you *want* to look for things to like in others you will be astonished how easy it is to find them.

Sometimes a compliment is most effective when you pay it to an unknown benefactor. I recall making a proposal to a group of fellow scientists. I could see that I had fluffed it; I oversold the proposal in my enthusiasm. But I did wind up my little talk with, "I do want to say a word of personal thanks to at least one among you who seemed to be sympathetic to my idea. I consider his interest and encouragement, silent as it was, complimentary enough to make me want to think this idea through and offer it later when it may have grown up a bit." Seven of the ten associates in that conference showed up in my office at varying times in the succeeding couple of days to tell me that *they* were my sympathetic though silent supporter!

5. The Tactful Way to Handle a Belligerent Neighbor

Perhaps we have been admonished to "love our neighbors" because at times it takes so much goodwill to get along with them, especially when they are the belligerent type.

When it comes to neighbor-relations or nation-relations, "war" is the approach that leaves both sides the losers.

One weekend while we were away, a neighbor of ours, who had been unfriendly to us ever since I refused to let him use our new power mower, decided to sneak it out of our garage. His idea was that he could get his grass cut and get the mower back into our garage before we got back. But his sneakiness got him into a pack of trouble.

This power mower would only work if the right gas-oil combination was used. My belligerent neighbor ran out of gas, so he filled up the mower with regular oil-free gasoline; then he couldn't get it started. This made him panicky. He rushed the mower off to the only repair shop in our area, but the repairman told him he was so busy that he couldn't fix it for him for at least a couple of days. With this, my neighbor returned the power mower to our garage and sat tight.

Later, when we went to use it, we found it would not work. So I brought it to the same repair shop, and when the repairman told me that somebody had tried to get him to fix the same power mower over the week end, it was easy to put two and two together.

Normally, such an infraction of private property would be justification for the declaration of a neighbor-war. I decided to use the tactful approach instead. Soon after the repairman had fixed the power mower (the carburetor had become fouled by the use of the wrong fuel mixture), I caught this neighbor's ear and explained to him all the mysterious trouble we had had with our power mower. He ducked the issue at first, but later broke down and explained the whole thing. Then, in his presence, I went about replacing the gasoline with the proper fuel and showed him how this particular mower really operated. Instead of getting mad, I told him that in the future he must never take anything out of our garage without clearing it with me and he understood, of course! The important point of this story is that if I had followed the alternative approach and accused him outright I would have incited a neighbor-war for life. As it turned out, little harm had been done, and this man has been one of the most wonderful neighbors we have ever known. A patient effort to help him "save face" made a friend instead of an enemy for life.

"Saving face" is said to be indispensable for the Chinese. But for the growth of goodwill, it is important everywhere to help others save face as often as possible. Saving face is the opposite of slapping it, and it has equally opposite results in helping you to success in all your dealings with others.

6. The Tactful Way to Open and Close Telephone Conversations

One man I know answers his telephone with the most unpleasant "Hello" imaginable. Basically, he is a wonderful fellow, but over the years he has handled a telephone as though the fellow on the other end were about to chew off his ear.

All of us use the telephone so much that good deportment here can be a valuable asset. A cheerful, happy, "Hello" can actually get a conversation off to the right start. Let the person calling you sense from the enthusiasm in your voice that you are glad to hear from him. A good procedure is to invite pleasantries by adding immediately after the introductions, "And what will you let me do for you?" or, if you haven't heard from the person in some time, "It is really delightful that you called!"

Equally important is the subtle use of tact to close a conversation on the telephone, especially the long-winded kind, which can eat into your work-day. "Let's pick this matter up again, soon," or, "If I didn't have to meet someone in five minutes, Harold, I'd love to go into this matter in further detail with you. How about getting together on this matter again, soon?"

7. The Tactful Way to Offset Deeply Personal Disappointments

Unfortunately, each of us at some time or another has had to break bad unpleasant news to others. On such occasions, it is especially important to go to the trouble of letting the person or persons involved know that you understand their problem as well as the meaning of the news you must give them.

A politician who is successful at getting reelected uses an extremely tactful way of handling his constituents' requests that he knows he cannot handle to their satisfaction. In one instance, when this official was forced to turn down a mother's request to try to have her son recalled from his assignment with NATO in Europe, he did so only after he was able to enclose with his reply a glowing report about her son from the colonel on whose staff he had been working.

A supervisor I know was faced with the problem of telling a man he highly regarded that an outsider had been hired to fill a spot above him. Before doing so, he assembled all the data he could about the experience and background of the newcomer, data which was impressive enough to assure his associate that the newcomer was eminently better qualified to fill the vacancy.

8. The Tactful Way to Round Out the Rough Spots in Your Marriage

Soon after Frank got married, he came to me all upset because he had begun to spot faults in his new bride that he had never suspected. He was shocked! What was he to do?

"Hold on" I advised Frank. "How do you know that your wife isn't equally shocked about you? It is not at all unusual for newlyweds to discover that 'all that glitters in each other is not gold.' If you want to save your marriage and mountains of heartbreaks you had better get to the root of your mutual dissatisfactions through the most tactful approach possible."

Frank followed my advice. Here is what he did. One evening when his wife, Sheila, was in what seemed to be a receptive frame of mind, he said to her: "Dear, now that we've been married several months, I am sure there are some things about me that you would like to see improved. Let's play a helpful game. Here are two sheets of paper. At the top of one is, "Improvements I would like to see in Frank" at the top of the other is, "Improvements I would like to see in Sheila."

They played the game and, to Frank's chagrin and enlightenment, Sheila's list was longer than his own! Both parties set their marriage right back on course as a result of this tactful look at each other, and now they are among the happiest couples we have the pleasure of knowing.

Tact is the best governor for human emotions. Use it to give others a shot in the arm without letting them feel the needle, to change them from porcupines into possums.

Before you administer criticism, give yourself the five-point test; take time to criticize yourself!

Learn, too, to paint sunsets instead of thunderclouds. Develop the eight practical ways to use tact in everyday life. Also, put these tact-active phrases to work in your behalf:

1. One of the nicest things you ever did for me was . . .
2. You would make me happy if . . .
3. Please be kind to . . .
4. I like the way you are able to put across so much in so few words . . .
5. Let's solve this problem together . . .
6. I can't wait to hear what you have to say about your . . .

Use tact in all your personal and business relationships and you will not fail to become increasingly strong in the power to influence the people in your life.

11.

How to Win Success
Through Friends

R EAL AND LASTING FRIENDSHIPS ARE AMONG THE
most neglected of human resources in America today. Most people on the treadmill to success realize too late that true security
lies not in money, but in genuine friends and friendships; not in
stocks and bonds and inflated bank accounts, but in the deepest
depths of human hearts; not in your own fame but in what you
do out of good will to help others and to let others help you! As
my father used to say, "The measure of a man's success in life is
not how much money he's made. It's the number and kind of
friends he can keep."

"Getting patronage," wrote George Bernard Shaw, "is the
whole art of life. A man cannot have a career without it." Just
how prepared are you to qualify for this "patronage" which
really means "the support of friends?" If you are to cultivate
friends and win the support of people who can help you to more
success and new advancements, you should be able to answer
with an unqualified "Yes" to each of the following questions. If
you cannot, then you should work or train yourself accordingly,

altering your outlook on life and people so that soon you will be
able to answer honestly "Yes" to those questions that you respond to with a "No" today.

1. Can you honestly look up to all your friends with a feeling
    of unenvious affection?

2. Do you always keep your estimation of a friend from sag-
    ging in the least just because a rumor about him reaches
    your ear when he is not around?

3. Can you take honest criticism from a friend without a
    surging desire to get even later?

4. Can you accept confidential information from a friend
    without the slightest thought of sharing it with somebody
    else?

5. Do you try to maintain an even keel of courtesy in your
    dealings with all your friends?

6. Do you prefer to say nothing about a person rather than
    repeat a truth that might lower him in the eyes of others?

7. Do you insist on "paying your way" with others, either
    with money or effort toward achieving a goal?

8. When you envision outstanding success, do you picture
    yourself as wanting to use your power to help your friends
    without any exception?

9. Can you take a joke, even when it might touch on the
    personal side—your looks or build, your mannerisms or
    your religious convictions—without feeling as if your ego
    has been mortally wounded?

10. When you make a promise to a friend, can you feel deep
    inside of you a willingness to endure sacrifices in order
    to keep it?

There is a very popular and successful man, Albert B., who
lived about a block from where I once lived. He has irresistible
charm. Albert could tell you about a long list of friends who have
done everything they could to make him as successful as he is.
Yet, I know that his success has grown only because he taught
himself, through years of discipline, the few simple rules that
are necessary to get other people to work wonders *for* you. Here
are the rules Albert follows:

1. He *always* talks in terms of what he can say in behalf of someone else or what he can do to bring real benefits to the other fellow.
2. He deliberately tries to win friends, many friends, the kind of whom he cannot have too many.
3. He works hard at acting like the kind of person he would like to be with ideally; Albert never has been known to start an argument, belittle a person's character or quirks, or set a depressing tone—he knows an optimistic one is always more contagious.
4. His conversation is loaded with remarks that will insure that neither his nor his listener's ego will be slighted!
5. He never has tried to force people to do or think anything. Albert knows that human beings who are made to assent outwardly will seldom, if ever, get over resenting inwardly.
6. Albert is as popular and successful as he is because people know the last thing he would ever do is cheat them out of the feeling of importance he knows they crave inwardly.
7. I heard him tell his secretary, when she complained because a certain member of the staff annoyed her by his domineering requests, "Half the battle in life is won as soon as you make up your mind that you will learn to get along with people who annoy you, because during half of your life, at least, they most certainly will."

First Law for Making Valuable Life-Long Friends

Many of us fail to realize that life for most people has its unbearable moments. You must face a constant parade of self-misgivings, temporary lapses of confidence, and momentary glimpses of failures and defeats. Each of us wants to be helped over life's rough spots, especially if we can get this help without losing "face" or faith in ourselves. And when this help also brings the best out in us, our debt of gratitude to the benefactor will remain clear in our minds all the way to the end of life's journey.

The first law for making valuable friends, then, is this: "Do everything in your power to increase the happiness and success of the other fellow." This law embodies the noblest moving forces in human beings. It is one of the richest, most powerful pieces of advice that can be taken to heart. By putting this law to work, you will make people hungry for your friendship. Once you can do this, you become a true millionaire in the noblest human sense.

The surest way to become unpopular and lose friends is to make the target of your aim to please yourself.

I know a young scientist, one whose career I have been able to follow rather closely since his graduation, who developed a few hard-hitting enemies shortly after he got his first job, by spilling his collegeitis over everyone within earshot. A really serious enemy that he made in this way was his first supervisor, who developed an intense dislike for him. Most unfortunately (it was all George's own fault), it took him twelve years to discover why this man disliked him and why the rate of his progress in his organization was much less than that to which he and many of his associates felt he was entitled. It was a pity that someone had not cautioned George about the dangers of making enemies in an organization while he was in college or very soon after he had left it. Starting one's first job with such mistakes can make or break your career at the outset!

George's case is a good illustration of the point that, if someone dislikes you, if you find your circle of friends narrowing down, it will pay you to double-check *yourself:* the chances are that the underlying causes are with you.

George's first supervisor was an older chemist, one who had been somewhat out of touch with the newer developments in the chemistry of man-made material. At conferences and discussions George, who was fresh from studying the latest textbooks, tactlessly spilled his fresh knowledge over everybody within earshot. George's supervisor had always been the one recognized authority in organic chemistry on the premises before George appeared. Yet everything George said, and his over-confident mannerisms, threw cold water on his supervisor's reputation. In other words, George's egotistical mannerism was about as smooth as sandpaper on his supervisor's ego.

Anytime such a situation is permitted to develop, you know

that a professed enemy has been made, or, even worse, a false friend, one who works against you behind an exterior of approval, may become added to your problems.

It was actually years later before George, somewhat mellowed now and more mature, was better able to appraise the true stature of his intellectual meagerness. Then he realized that it was his display of superficially superior knowledge that caused his supervisor to become a serious roadblock to his progress.

Having reached this conclusion in his self-appraisal, George deliberately began to untie the unfriendly knot into which he had literally tied himself almost twelve years before. He was very successful at it, and today there are few persons who say nicer things behind George's back than this supervisor.

But the road back for George was a most difficult one. He succeeded only by painfully and patiently building up his supervisor's reputation so that once again it became like a shining star above George's own reputation. It was not until the supervisor repeatedly received word by the grapevine that George was now his champion that the wind began to blow favorably in George's direction. Then, this one-time enemy of George's became his most valuable friend. This man's vote was sufficient, at the appropriate time, to disqualify an outside contender for the important job that George now has as director of a laboratory.

KNOW YOUR ENEMIES—THEN DISCOUNT THEM!

Abraham Lincoln probably ranks second to none in the skill with which any man has been able to destroy his enemies. The classic example, of course, was the manner in which he never missed an occasion to speak kindly of the South despite the bitter animosities of the Civil War. When one of his supporters called him on this policy and attitude, President Lincoln calmly turned to him and said, "There are two ways to destroy your enemies; one is by brute force. By this method, neither of you really win; both of you are hurt. The better way to destroy an enemy is by changing your enemy into a true friend."

Abe Lincoln was a master proponent of the philosophy to be successful, you cannot have too many friends; to be successful, you cannot afford to have a single enemy.

An elderly businessman I knew told me, "Always remember that one enemy is too many. Never be afraid of those enemies who are outspoken and leave no room for doubt that they are your enemies. With these you can cope because you know where you stand with them. It is the hidden enemy, like the hidden tax, that erodes from within."

It is of the utmost importance that you appreciate, right from the start, the truth that you cannot expect to go through life without having enemies, enemies of many shades and shadows. As one man has quipped, "There are many people who believe they have no enemies, but the fact of the matter is that practically all of their friends hate them!"

Nevertheless, your ability to make friends out of enemies can mean the difference between success and failure for you. The problem of making friends out of enemies is, of course, an age-old one. "Agree with your adversary quickly," is one time-tested formula for handling this universal problem. Your chances of becoming popular and successful, of winning the "patronage" of friends, without this basic approach to people are most unfavorable.

Getting an enemy to do you a favor is one way to plant the seed of lasting friendship in forbidden territory. For example, at one time we lived next door to a very unfriendly neighbor. The chances are he had reasons of his own to distrust us and to believe that we were not friendly. Certainly our growing children may have used some sticks and stones to help encourage his obvious feeling of animosity.

But one day we learned quite indirectly that this rather sour-faced, unhappy neighbor had a heart condition. He had been warned by his physician never to shovel any snow. When the next heavy snowstorm came our way, I spent an extra fifteen minutes clearing his sidewalk. When spring came along, I did rake the twigs and dead leaves from some of his property alongside of our own. I even cleaned up and trimmed the shrubbery. I did these things not knowing for sure whether they would be noticed by him.

In any event, I knew that this man was an engineer for a

plumbing supply house. One day that spring our hot-water heater sprang a leak. It was a week end and, in desperation, I approached this man for help. I approached him as though he was the only person in the whole world who could lead us out of our predicament.

He came enthusiastically, almost too enthusiastically, down our cellar stairs, walked to a valve and turned the water off. My wife and I smiled in admiration as the spray of water which had been pouring out of a pinpoint hole in the hot water tank slumped to a mere drip.

"You'll need a new boiler," he told me with the attitude of a physician announcing a successful diagnosis. "But until you can get a plumber, I'll plug this leak for you."

Letting that man do me a favor was like pouring oil on angry waves. We became real friends and pleasant neighbors. We enjoyed their strawberries and they enjoyed our flowers. I used his ladder and he used my wheelbarrow. What's most important, we smiled at each other, even talked a blue streak at times over the back fence.

True friendship must, of course, be far and above any selfish interests. Anytime the business of friendship becomes tainted with selfish motives, it leads to unhappy endings.

Real friends, after all, are: (1) Folks who know your faults, but boast about your good points. (2) People who would not say anything about you behind your back that they would not say to your face. (3) Folks who have shared joys and sorrows with you. (4) People who have fortified you in times of trial.

Without friends to enliven your life with rich and varied experiences, to help you bring to the surface those better qualities that lay hidden deep inside you, the going can be bitter and unbearable, even in this day of atomic energy, space ships, and satellites. As one retired man told me, and he spoke for the majority of retired men and women with whom I have talked, "There are some kinds of friends we cannot have too many of. The secret of true happiness, of real success and influence in dealing with people, lies in finding more than a normal share of them."

Inasmuch as knowing how to make friends on the job can be so important to you, let us examine the more common situations in a variety of occupations where friends and your approach to the making of friends can have widely different end results.

One man I know has created numerous enemies (or at least unfriendly friends) and received less cooperation in turn, not because he was incompetent or basically unpleasant to work with, but because he had a most annoying mannerism on the telephone. His telephone deportment was just the type of thing to start a conversation off on the wrong foot. When you heard his gruff, blunt "Hello," your first thought was to say "Good-bye."

This same person had many little annoying idiosyncrasies, all of which put him at a great disadvantage in his efforts to progress. He invariably asked questions in such a way that he gave you the impression that he already knew you did not or could not possibly know the answers! He would explain something quickly and then, after a moment's pause, curtly say, "Don't you understand what I mean?" This man had few real friends on the job despite the fact that he was a man of principles and unusual honesty and integrity.

When it comes to trying to make friends, the sooner you learn the following approach followed by a top executive, the sooner you will be moving up the ladder to success, no matter what kind of work you do.

The man I am thinking of is best known for what you might call the proven "toned down" or "de-egoed" approach. For example, here are some of his stock questions and comments that you also might use to advantage:

1. Do you really think this might work?
2. Would you mind helping me out of this little difficulty?
3. I'm sure you understand this, but I can't quite figure it out. Would you explain it for me?
4. I've always respected your judgment on problems like this.
5. I'll bet you can get this little job done before lunch.
6. Your honesty is downright invigorating.
7. No one could ever accuse you of not being company-minded.
8. That's the way to make a problem evaporate.

This leading executive probably learned over a period of years that the secret of winning other people to your side is literally to put your arm around their shoulders and bring them in on your problems wholeheartedly. He told me once that no matter how smart a person or how hard he may work he cannot get anywhere alone.

Even in the exceptional cases of successful "loners," he who travels alone may travel farther and faster, as the Chinese say, but not with as much fun and pleasure as he who travels slower but with good companions.

FRIENDS AND FRIENDSHIPS: CONTRIBUTED STATEMENTS BY THREE OF AMERICA'S TOP BUSINESS LEADERS

In the course of writing this book, I invited several prominent Americans to give you their thoughts on the art of making friends and the value that this art can be to you. Here are the exclusive statements they gave me for use in this book. They are well worth repeated study by all of us who realize, with St. John Ervine, "To be able to say that you have a friend is to know that there is one person to whom your affairs are as important as his own, on whose aid and counsel and affection you can count in all times of trouble and distress, to whose aid you will fly the moment you hear he needs your help."

Conrad N. Hilton, President, Hilton Hotels:

When I think about friendship I am reminded of a religious order existing in Europe during the middle ages. Its members were known as the Friends of God. They sought holiness not in creeds or ceremonies, but in union and fellowship with God.

And I am reminded that our word *friend* comes from an ancient Gothic verb that meant 'to love.' In the Burmese language the root of the word 'a friend' is the same as that of the word 'a relative.'

Thus, the world over, a friend is someone very close to you—someone to love, esteem and respect. Friendship is a relationship freely given, an affection freely sought or granted. Though it may carry responsibilities, it is never an obligation. Perhaps that is why true friendship is always so wonderful.

John E. McKeen, President, Chas. Pfizer & Co., Inc.:

Some of the wisest counsel ever given on the subject of friends and friendships was stated succinctly by Ralph Waldo Emerson. He said that the only way to have a friend is to be one. And this guide to friendship is just as valid today as it was in Emerson's time.

Will Rogers used to say that he never met a man he didn't like. Not everyone has been as fortunate as Mr. Rogers, but it would mark the baseness of a man were he to dislike a person before he had a chance to know him. All true friendships must be based on the dignity of the individual and this spirit can operate only in the absence of prejudice and ignorance.

If a friend is worth choosing, he is worth helping, and people will find rare pleasure in working together to serve someone else's needs. The time and counsel given may better the wide world around us and any skill so acquired is a reward in itself.

Walter Annenberg, Editor and Publisher, The Philadelphia Inquirer:

I have found that life can offer few more genuine satisfactions than those which derive from true friendships. Good friends, honest friends should be guarded and treasured among one's most priceless possessions. Beyond any other measure, they are the real hallmark of a successful human being.

CHAPTER ELEVEN IN REVIEW

If you aim to win success through friends, you must make *them* your target, not yourself. In other words, the first law that will help you to win true friends, of whom you cannot have too many, is this: "Do Everything in Your Power To Increase the Happiness and Success of The Other Fellow!"

Abraham Lincoln knew that *one* enemy in life is too many: "There are two ways to destroy your enemies; one is by brute force. By this method, neither of you really win; both of you are hurt. The better way to destroy an enemy is by changing your enemy into a true friend."

Beware, too, of falling into the trap of believing that you have no enemies, when in fact you may be deserving of the animosity of all your friends.

Learn the eight Friend-Making Phrases and put them to work in making friends on the job, around the community, even within your family.

Finally, can you, in order to win friends who will help you to greater success:

1. Guard confidences?
2. Take a clear-cut stand when the reputation of a friend is challenged?
3. Suppress a feeling of envy or superiority?
4. Keep your promises?
5. Never try to oversell yourself to them?
6. Give and take with them willingly?
7. Cherish them as delicate jewels you will not drop?
8. Take honest criticism without a surging urge to retaliate?
9. Maintain an even keel of courtesy with all your friends?
10. Insist on paying your way with others, either with money or effort?

12.

The Ten Principles of Influencing and Dealing With People

---

1. SPEAK EVIL OF NO ONE

THIS FIRST PRINCIPLE OF SUCCESS IN DEALING WITH people is the cornerstone around which the other nine principles must be grouped. The urge to criticize, to belittle, to defame, to hurt others is a universal weakness of human nature. Your ability to overwhelm this undercurrent of human behavior grows out of a rigid policy of refusing to speak evil of anyone.

In applying this crucial pillar to successful human relations in your own life, you may well use as your model, Rex, an outstandingly popular executive and community leader. Almost every day, it seems, I run into a person who directly or indirectly brings out the basic importance of Rex's unrelenting adherence to this principle of influencing others—Speak Evil of No One.

Let us examine Rex more closely to see how he lives this principle to the full. The following quotations by Rex, as well as specific situations in which he has practiced this first principle, come to my mind spontaneously. He has such a clean-cut popularity rating with me (and with countless other persons too) that

I never have had to keep careful notes about him. The things he says and does all have an indelibleness about them, remaining fresh in spite of time or a diminishing memory:

1. "The next time you have a morsel of biting information about a neighbor or an associate," I heard Rex tell a fellow employee, "stop your tongue speechless in its groove. Refuse to mention it even to your wife or your best friend. Soon the urge to tell it, and the newsworthiness of the tidbit will fade away, and you'll find an extra morsel of life creep into your body for having done so."

2. It was a convention of chemists in Chicago; Rex and I were in the same group. We were seated around a table having lunch. One of the persons in the group tried to focus the conversation on a certain vice-president who, it was rumored, was going to "get the gate."

   "I always thought J. P. was nothing but a windbag" said the purveyor of the uncouth bit of gossip, "and I'm glad to see the bag is finally getting punctured!"

   Rex got into the conversation before others could pick up this remark, add to it, endorse it, and thereby damage themselves as well as do the vice-president in question an unretractable injustice.

   "'Cut it!" Rex interjected with a firmness he was known to use only on the rarest of occasions; "J. P. is a friend of mine." Then, with his usual bubbling, friendly enthusiasm, he shifted the conversation to an exciting new discovery he had heard about during a morning lecture.

Weeks later, Rex's action at this luncheon came back to me, and the underlying stature of his position was revealed. J. P., whom one of the men in the luncheon party was tempted to belittle on the basis of a threadbare rumor, was promoted to the presidency of a firm with which his parent company had since merged. Rex knew that this move was in the wind when an attempt was made to attack J. P.'s character that day at the luncheon. As it turned out, too, the man who tried to assail J. P.'s character worked for the company J. P. now heads. The "windbag" he permitted himself the luxury of trying to burst is now his boss! Imagine how much harm he could have done himself if his attempt to slur J. P. really picked up a full head of gossip-steam and made its way to J. P. himself. Rex did this man a real favor by helping to nip in the bud his urge to "speak some evil" about another.

3. Favorite expressions that Rex uses when he talks about people are:

"John is a solid fellow, so solid I would trust him with a blank check over my signature."

"The nice thing about that fellow is the way he shows you he wants to help you more than he wants to help himself."

"I have yet to find anything about George that I didn't like."

"Someday Bill will develop the polish he needs."

"The Smiths are a wonderful family. You know every time we spend an evening with them we return home feeling that this wobbly old planet still has some good and wonderful inhabitants on it."

If you learn to go around with a "speak no evil" outlook like Rex's, your popularity and influence can't do anything but grow, and grow luxuriantly. Try putting this principle into practice. You will be astonished by the results you will see and feel. These results will make you as devoted to the practice of Principle One as is Rex himself.

In the words of the great Will Durant, "Speak no evil of anyone, every unkind word will sooner or later fly back into your face, and make you stumble in the race of life. To speak ill of others is a dishonest way of praising ourselves; let us be above such transparent egotism. If you can't say good and encouraging things, say nothing. Nothing is often a good thing to do, and always a clever thing to say."

2. NEVER SEEK *PERSONAL* GAIN AT THE EXPENSE OF SOMEBODY ELSE

Principle Number Two has a way of creeping into your behavior with the stealthiness of a termite. It is well worth a careful examination of conscience regularly to make sure you are not violating it.

Take the case of Warren. His boss, Jack, was away on a two-week vacation, and he was placed in temporary charge. A vice-president called him for some information that his boss had been asked to get. Warren mistakingly thought that this was an opportunity to impress the "big boss."

"Jack was hoping you wouldn't ask for this information until he got back," Warren told the vice-president. "It will be no trouble for me to get it for you and I'll get a memo off to you about it this afternoon." A subtle dig at his boss! But not really a glowing plug for himself. Warren revealed a most unflattering trait when he failed to defend his own boss in his absence. The other fellow can tell instinctively when you are trying to feather your own nest at somebody else's expense. When he does, you end up filling your nest with spikes instead of feathers!

Imagine how impressed the vice-president would have been with Warren if he had given this reply:

"Jack was rounding this data up for you just before he left for vacation. He was overwhelmed with last-minute work and asked me to be sure to get the information ready for you. I will get a memorandum out to you in the afternoon mail giving you the complete story you want."

Warren's popularity with a vice-president of his firm would have been insured for life if he had followed this latter approach. His subtle attempt for personal gain at his boss's expense, on the other hand, became a roadblock in his path to success. The vice-president he talked to would always have some misgivings about giving Warren 100 per cent support if and when an occasion requiring it arose.

3. LIVE TODAY—AND DEPOSIT YOUR WORRIES IN THE BANK OF TOMORROW

It was the great physician, Sir William Osler, who constantly advised his emotionally tense patients to "live in daytight compartments." To live this advice you must teach yourself to worry about important things first, and only one at a time.

Elizabeth, an elderly widow, stands out in my mind as one person who has always "lived in daytight compartments." Despite an endless string of setbacks and sorrows that have marked her life, she stands at eighty-three erect in posture, sharp in sight and mind, and warm and kindly in disposition.

Her formula for "living today," especially when clouds hang heavy overhead, is to dig into work for others:

(1) Her daughter was to undergo a serious operation; instead of worrying for several hours in a hospital waiting room, she brought along a petit point for a piano seat cover. She worked on this painstaking job so energetically while she waited for the nurse to let her come in to see her daughter that she could not let her mind dwell on what was or what was not being done to her little girl on the operating table.

(2) Her son was flying home from a business trip; the weather was bad. In anticipation of his plane being overdue she busied herself making a couple of lemon meringue pies, the kind of pies her son was crazy about.

(3) If some event came along to create an air of tenseness throughout the household, she would whip together a team of every able-bodied person on hand and direct them as a "gang" in doing a bang-up housecleaning job on the basement or the attic.

These examples are described only to give you an insight into Elizabeth's zest for *living today* through action, which she pursues especially when the reverberations of yesterday or the qualms of tomorrow attempt to make inroads into the joy of living today to the full. Basically, her success in life comes from a strict adherence to the principle that a day spent in activity of any kind is a day better spent than one of brooding and moping.

By so handling the inevitable low points of her busy life, Elizabeth has become all the more wonderful and all the more liked during the equally inevitable high spots of her life. Sunday dinners at her house were often like an outdoor church picnic. Everybody was welcome, and the easiest thing in the world for Elizabeth seemed to be to find an extra plate and an extra chair for a newcomer.

Of all the people I have known I do believe that she possesses the best grasp of the wonderful principle to popularity, and success—*LIVE TODAY.*

4. AVOID HURT FEELINGS AT ALL COSTS

Probably the least charitable of all human reactions is that of refusing to forgive. It is so sad to see and hear of people who, because of a single hurt, will go through year after year of hatred and bitterness toward the person who caused the hurt.

Because human beings are so sensitive to hurt feelings, and because there are few human beings who can shrug off an insult or an injustice, you can do your popularity and influence with others a lasting disservice each time you inadvertently or otherwise hurt another person's feelings.

I recall an instance when an older brother "bawled out" his younger brother mercilessly. He did so in what he thought was a spirit of helpfulness. The younger brother wanted someday to be a banker, but as a senior in college he still was slipshod in his posture and dress. The older brother, a meticulous engineer, dressed him down one day before giving him some financial assistance. But he pressed his criticism so far that he hurt the pride of the younger brother deeply.

The younger brother did begin to keep his shoes shined, his pants pressed, and his hair combed. But his ego had been hurt by a tactless dressing-down and he would never forget it as long as he lived.

Time marched on and the younger brother, now dapper in his Homburg, gloves, and velvet-collared dress coat, became a wealthy banker. The older brother, although a successful engineer, developed arthritis and eventually was forced to go to the younger brother for financial help. Now the tables were turned, but the wound the younger brother suffered had not really healed over the years. All he could remember was his hurt pride, perhaps the precise stimulus that drove him on to success. He helped his brother, but only by making him pay a price, the price of refusing to forgive him!

Life is replete with many fateful family feuds that grew out of petty hurt feelings. The same kind of feuds develop on the job, and in social and community life. Each and every one of them grows, like a mushroom, from a tiny spore, that of a hurt feeling.

Try to be like a certain popular clergyman I know, and you

never will live to regret violating the fourth principle to successful dealings with people. He firmly believes that you should do everything within your power to prevent a single hurt feeling.

"It is within your power and mine," he said in a recent conversation with me, "to feel kindly toward others, especially when their actions deserve to be criticized. A single gesture of understanding always brings better results than an open criticism of another, no matter how called for the criticism may appear to be on the surface. It still is better to influence others by letting your light so shine before men that they may, in seeing your good works, come to see their own weakness themselves." Anyone who follows this advice in his dealings with people will never get himself into the sad predicament of righteous indignation which breeds hurt feelings.

Here are two keys to avoid hurting the other fellow's feelings, keys that can open your door to greater power in influencing people.

1. *Use persuasion and inspiration instead of criticism to put across your points or to correct another person's errors.*

My clergyman-friend told me that when he learns that a couple in his parish is on the verge of breaking up due to marital discord, he looks for them at church, and, when he sees them in the congregation either alone or together, he deliberately switches the theme of his prepared sermon to emphasize the sacredness of the marriage vows: for better or for worse, for richer or for poorer, in sickness and in health, until death do us part. He follows this with a particularly effective five minute talk on the responsibilities of partners in marriage. "In this way," he told me, "without endangering supersensitive personal feelings, I know I have been able through indirect persuasion and inspiration to cement many a loosening marital bond together again."

2. *Never act snobbish, conceited, or unapproachable to people.*

One of the most popular scientists in the nation today is a dynamic man who forever beams cordiality wherever he goes. He keeps one of two secretaries almost constantly busy writing letters of admiration or appreciation for his signature. His smile and his hand are always wide open.

Compare this popular man with the introvert and unpopular company president who deems it below his dignity to talk with the hired help. Despite all the print to the contrary, such individuals do continue to exist in actual practice. They can be found in many so-called "modern" companies, occupying chairs at descending levels from the presidential offices, also.

Conceit and snobbishness are utterly incompatible with popularity, influence, and long-lived success. Beware of them.

It has been said that people generally have poor memories. This may be true when it comes to remembering debts or anniversaries. But there is one thing of which you can be sure, when it comes to remembering old grudges, humiliations, rejections, or buried hatreds: the other fellow at least, should be counted on as having a perfect and, most unfortunately at times, indelible memory.

5. LOVE LIFE AND PEOPLE OPENLY

Love others for their sake as well as for your own. Refuse to give hate a chance to get even its foot in the door of your innermost emotions. Hate is a poison that quickly vitiates your character and causes your personality to degenerate.

In a nutshell, the best formula for successful human relations ever written still revolves about learning to love your neighbor, not for his looks, smile, or bank account, but because he is a fellow human being. This is the primary guidepost on how to get along with *everybody* as well as how to have influence and be successful with people. It is a policy that cannot be improved upon. The man who learns to love life and people openly, wholeheartedly, and honestly cannot help but stand out like a new dime in a fish bowl of dull pennies.

6. SERVE OTHERS UNSELFISHLY: THERE IS NO BETTER WAY TO INFLUENCE PEOPLE

"No one can be a self-contained entity" Charles F. Kettering once told me. "You are either going to serve somebody or be a servant to somebody if you are going to contribute anything to the world in which we live."

Sit back and reflect on the most influential people in history or in your life today. "Service to others" will be the common denominator that has firmly cemented together the reputations of each and everyone of them from St. Francis of Assisi to Florence Nightingale, from Louis Pasteur to Jonas Salk, from the president of America's most successful corporation to that jovial shoeshine boy who does an extra-special job on your shoes!

Adolph, for example, is a person who has completely grasped the role of service as a means of making his life more wholesome. He is only a janitor, to be sure, but he is not an ordinary janitor. There is something special about Adolph and he has dozens and dozens of friends who could talk to you at some length about him.

The zest with which he has performed services for people time and again has eased the furrowed brows of tense executives, or a smog-bound mental *impasse* of a hard-thinking research chemist. Not only does Adolph show you he wants to be of service; he takes the time to do the undemanded things that prove his point:

1. When he empties an ash tray on your desk, he never places it down again until he has wiped it crystal-clean.
2. Any time he sees pencils lying around that need sharpening, he sharpens them without being asked.
3. Desk calendars are set like magic, and office blackboards are never without a clean brush and plenty of chalk.
4. At quitting time, if it happens to be showering and you are especially worried about getting a new straw hat drenched, the chances are that Adolph will appear beside you with one of several abandoned umbrellas he has collected over the years.
5. Adolph, with his ever-warm smile, seems always to be trying to figure out what you could possibly want him to do for you. And it is amazing how frequently his quick eye or his intuition can anticipate your wishes.

Is Adolph a popular fellow? I had no idea of the extent of his influence and the real measure of his success at the type of work he had measured out for himself, until word got around one day that his ten-year-old son was in the hospital. He had been accidentally hit by a car and was in urgent need of large supplies of blood.

Notices did not have to be sent around asking for volunteers. The company president was among the first to volunteer because he happened to have the particular blood-type needed! Furthermore, the cards, the flowers, and the personal expressions of condolence that came from all directions, from top brass and bottom bronze, swamped Adolph's emotions.

Popular? Successful? Adolph's devotion to service for others has built up a universal attachment towards him among his associates that must be seen to be fully appreciated. He taught me and, I am sure, countless other people that the part of yourself you give away in the service of others is, in the last analysis, the only part of yourself that you really will keep forever. Unselfish service is the lifeline to the kind of lasting influence that spreads its roots deep in the hearts of others. This kind of influence does not wither easily. Like the treasures you store up in heaven, it resists the rust and tarnish of even the least charitable elements among human beings.

7. KEEP YOUR SIGHTS ON THE OTHER PERSON'S DRIVES

Most people completely ignore what "drives" the other fellow because they are so taken up with trying to drive themselves! Is it any wonder that they have head-on collisions?

The best drivers are those who watch the other motorists as though each were a moron; they keep alert for every sign or clue as to what the other driver intends to do and then they steer their own car accordingly.

The same policy can be applied when it comes to preventing head-on collisions with the other fellow's emotions. Yet, I dare say, most of us give much less serious thought to figuring out the other fellow's drives than we do to selecting our favorite brand of cigarettes. Yet, it is the fellow who figures out why the other fellow *will* do things, why he *wants* to do things, that has perfect command of any situation.

Jerry is a fellow who keeps asking himself this question a dozen times a day: "How can I make him (or her) want to do this for me?" He will tell you he got his cue for this principle of power in dealing with people from Henry Ford I who said, "If there is any one secret of success it lies in the ability to get the other person's point of view and see things from his angle as well as your own."

Jerry applies this principle of "Keeping Your Sight on the Other Person's Drive" in the following ways:

1. Mr. Q., a well-known author, is noted in his community for his blank refusal to give talks before groups of any kind. As program chairman of his local Lions Club, Jerry makes up his mind that he is going to get Mr. Q. to speak at one of his luncheon dates. So, the first thing he does is ask himself, "What might a man like Mr. Q. have his sights on these days?" After some thought, Jerry decided he might be on the right track.

He recalled having seen a complimentary review of Mr. Q.'s most recent book in a back issue of The Lion Magazine. He dug it up and sent the clipping to Mr. Q. in the belief that he would be interested in it and that he may have missed seeing it. Of course, Jerry added his own appreciation of the book, having read it from cover to cover!

Back came a wonderful note of appreciation from Mr. Q. Hard on the heels of this note, Jerry called Mr. Q. on the telephone and told him that his Lions Club had been hoping for years to be favored by a twenty-minute talk by him. Would he please oblige them and be their guest speaker at the annual dinner-dance next month? Jerry got his speaker. The Club attributed it to Jerry's super-magnetic personality.

2. On another occasion, Jerry was puzzled as to how he could help his wife lose ten pounds without giving her the slightest idea that the middle-age spread was beginning to detract from her figure. He knew she had tried dieting a dozen times and had spent a small fortune on all kinds of reducing fads. Once again, he sought a drive in his wife on which he could capitalize.

One day he hit upon the formula, one that had a double-barrelled benefit. His wife was especially proud to be seen in the community with him. He was a successful man; what's more, his wife thought he was a mighty attractive man to be out with.

Realizing that he himself was not getting the exercise he should, Jerry suggested to his wife that they take an invigorating post-dinner walk together each evening. It worked like magic.

Each evening, soon after the dishwasher was on its way, Jerry's wife appeared in her walking shoes, all prettied up for her invigorating walk with her dark-haired, pipe-smoking husband. After the first few evenings of about a two-mile workout over the streets of their beautiful suburban community, Jerry and his wife found their breath coming easier, and within six weeks Jerry could see that he had his wife's weight down to the point where it was just right for him, at least. And his wife loved him all the more as a result of Jerry's initiative to provide this pleasant companionship after a busy day apart.

These two examples explain why perhaps everybody who knows Jerry says, "He's such a wonderful fellow. He's so easy to get along with. It is a pleasure to figure out a way to do him a little favor now and then."

8. NEVER GIVE YOUR WORD OR MAKE A PROMISE YOU CANNOT KEEP OR BACK UP

"Always keep a promise or your word, son," my father once advised me. "A broken promise or a broken word is as hard to repair as a broken mirror!"

Perhaps the best way to adhere to this principle is to avoid making careless and unnecessary promises. This is a trap into which a supervisor, for example, or a parent can easily fall.

Jack was a department head who had a reputation for going to bat for the people who worked under him, and usually he could strike a home run for them. But he did get himself into some tight, uncomfortable, and unpopular spots at times. In one instance, he had assured an employee that he was going to get a $500 a year raise. He had, it was true, signed the salary recommendation, but he committed himself to this employee in a weak moment even though the raise would not be official until it received the endorsement of the salary committee. Imagine Jack's sad plight when word came to him that a recent decision of the Board of Directors to cut the quarterly dividend in half carried with it a moratorium on all salary increases for at least six months!

If you will make a careful study of the matter, you will observe that most people are constantly making careless and unnecessary promises. George was just the opposite of Jack in this respect. He had a solid reputation for keeping his word and never over-extending his promises. When I asked him for some tips based on his experiences with this principle, here is what he told me:

1. Learn to say "Yes" or "No" promptly and decisively in life. People will respect you more when they know you mean what you say. So many times a person gives a hesitant "no," ending up with a more uncertain "yes," especially when they are asked to do something such as give a talk, collect for the Red Cross in the neighborhood block, or even help out at a Boy Scout meeting. The people who have the hardest time keeping their word or their promises are those who, through undecision, always end up biting off more than they can chew with a reasonable effort. In the end, such persons lose the respect, and confidence of others, and their reputation sours, even though they may expend much more energy trying to keep a hesitant promise than the fellow who says "Yes" or "No" decisively.

2. Be a clock-watcher when it comes to keeping appointments. Some of the most important men in *Who's Who* would be upset if they were ten or fifteen minutes late for a scheduled appointment.

Have you ever had to wait for somebody a half-hour or more beyond the appointed meeting time? Do you recall how a negative reaction developed toward the tardy party while you were twiddling your thumbs? The same deflation of your own position occurs, of course, when you allow yourself the shallow pleasure of being tardy. You cannot expect to exert much influence over people who have you pegged as a time waster, someone who does not respect his commitments.

3. If you are a person in charge of a household or a group of people, beware of making loose promises. The children will never forget that you let them down if you don't come good with that trip to California or Hawaii; your wife will resent not having that new fur coat you promised her, even jokingly, each time

she sees a friend wearing one; that employee will develop a dislike for you if the raise, promotion, or transfer you told him or her you were pushing for falls through.

George's points are all extremely illustrative of the importance of making your word as good as your bond. Nothing will build up your power to influence people more than a feeling of solid trust and confidence in your words and deeds on the part of everyone you know and with whom you deal.

9. TREASURE YOUR HEALTH—TAKE ALL THE TIME YOU NEED TO KEEP WELL

It is absurd, but there are numerous graveyards wherein lie those short-lived meteors who enjoyed success and popularity for a brief moment, only to realize too late they had ruined their "bearings" and as a result, burned out their hearts.

Success without good health, apart from its short-livedness, is like eating food without tasting the flavor. Few sins of Americans in pursuit of success are more obvious than the flagrant disrespect people on the road to success show their bodies.

Business men on lush expense accounts lop years off their success-life by drinking and eating excessively.

Young fellows aspiring to get ahead *fast* try to do it too fast by upsetting the proper and vital balance between work and play.

Even young mothers, overanxious to do an outstanding job raising a famliy, prod themselves into becoming premature mental and physical derelicts by taking their jobs too seriously without sufficient care for their own minds and bodies.

The record of the few who can hold their health and the reigns of their success well into old age is one that is constantly similar to that of a sixty-four-year-old president of a chemical company I know. This man is a millionaire, owning an estate on which you could easily build an eighteen-hole golf course.

On the job, he has the reputation of being a fireball. Nobody in his company keeps hours more punctually. Nobody can claim to be a harder worker. But what are the facts behind this man's secret of balancing good health with sustained success? Here they are:

1. His wife told me that during the past thirty years it has been the exception rather than the rule for her husband to retire after 11:00 P.M.

2. This man spends his entire week ends in relative solitude on his estate but also in outdoor physical activity: he prunes his peach trees, digs the weeds out of his strawberry patch, mows some of his lawn, even cultivates some of the land in the spring!

3. Even more important, early in his climb to the top, he curbed his weight and never did allow himself to start growing in the middle. In his younger years, he went skiing a week at a time, square-danced, and sailed his boat just to keep in good health.

4. He loves good music and has taken in every significant Broadway musical. During the winter, unless business calls him out of the city, you can find this man with his wife relaxing to the music of the Philadelphia Orchestra, for he has bought season tickets for decades.

5. And, on top of all these efforts on his part to take good care of his health, once a year like clock-work he has an old friend of his at Temple University Hospital go over him with a fine-tooth comb. These annual physicals have added more years to his popularity and success than all of his other efforts combined. Here's why:

(a) When he was forty-five, a tiny suspicious growth was spotted and removed from beside his nose.

(b) At forty-seven, a tendency toward hemorrhoids was noted and corrected.

(c) At fifty, a temporary upswing in his blood pressure due to a serious drop in his company's profit was tided over with the aid of proper medication.

(d) At fifty-five, special exercises were indicated to preclude a very slight warning that varicose veins might be forming.

(e) At sixty, another suspicious growth, this time under his little toe, was removed as a safety measure.

At sixty-four, this man is a wonderful example of a typical

successful, healthy American business man. His constant vigilance about his health has paid off handsomely. Although many of his associates passed on at forty-five, fifty or fifty-five, he remained skipper of his ship, growing in wealth, satisfaction, popularity, and influence all the while in his dealings with an ever-widening circle of friends.

This principle of "Treasuring Your Health" is the one that governs the amount of time during which you will enjoy the benefits of your ability to influence others successfully. It may be true that "A life well-spent is a long life," but in our modern day when competition has all but eliminated the chance to rocket overnight to the top, good health over as many years as possible is the most vital requirement for building up a lasting pyramid of success in dealing with people. As a matter of record, a recent extensive survey among wage-earning adults showed conclusively that what they wanted *most* out of life was continued good health. Significantly, this poll showed that their second most intense interest in life was, in essence, what this book has tried to help you to achieve—the skill in handling human beings in order to get along well with them, earn their respect, and win their cooperation and influence.

10. THINK, THINK, THINK THAT YOU WILL BE SUCCESSFUL IN YOUR DEALINGS WITH PEOPLE

There are two common ways that people mistakenly look upon success:

(1) They feel they are successful as soon as they are sure that *others* look upon *them* as being very successful.

(2) They assume they are successful because they feel *superior* to others.

The man or woman who falls prey to the second idea of success soon finds it is suicidal, literally self-destructive. Real success and influence can only be built upon a recognition that they, like every good thing in this life, are willingly given to you or recognized by others with their willingness, initiative, and consent.

The great Apostle Paul, upon the occasion of his striking conversion to a better way of life, had the soundest advice I have been able to find anywhere on how to become successful in dealing with people. What he wrote to his friends can be summed up as follows:

"I am going to live a noble life from this day forward, because I *think* I can."

Paraphrasing the familiar saying about prayer, "More dreams come true than people ever *think* possible," the most dynamic truth is that, as Paul, you too can ultimately live a noble, successful, and influential life, if you will constantly and confidently *think, know* you can. A corollary of this is the resolution, "I will do my best in everything and keep *thinking* I will succeed in doing my best." Such a principle will keep you doing the truly important things, while the little things will take care of themselves.

A quotation by the immortal Ralph Waldo Emerson hangs in my office, and it seems like a most fitting way to summarize this book. In sharing it with you, it is my hope that you will find it as invaluable to you as it has been to me:

"To laugh often and love much; to win the respect of intelligent people and the affection of children; to earn the approbation of honest critics and endure the betrayal of false friends; to appreciate beauty; to find the best in others; to give one's self; to leave the world a bit better, whether by a healthy child, a garden patch, or a redeemed social condition; to have played and laughed with enthusiasm and sung with exultation; to know even one life has breathed easier because you have lived—this is to have succeeded."

Index

Index